Sun Signs

Secrets of Star Sign Astrology, Sun-Moon Astrology Combinations, Your Personality Type, and More

© Copyright 2022 - All rights reserved.

The content contained within this book may not be reproduced, duplicated, or transmitted without direct written permission from the author or the publisher.

Under no circumstances will any blame or legal responsibility be held against the publisher, or author, for any damages, reparation, or monetary loss due to the information contained within this book, either directly or indirectly.

Legal Notice:

This book is copyright protected. It is only for personal use. You cannot amend, distribute, sell, use, quote, or paraphrase any part, or the content within this book, without the consent of the author or publisher.

Disclaimer Notice:

Please note the information contained within this document is for educational and entertainment purposes only. All effort has been executed to present accurate, up-to-date, reliable, and complete information. No warranties of any kind are declared or implied. Readers acknowledge that the author is not engaging in the rendering of legal, financial, medical, or professional advice. The content within this book has been derived from various sources. Please consult a licensed professional before attempting any techniques outlined in this book.

By reading this document, the reader agrees that under no circumstances is the author responsible for any losses, direct or indirect, that are incurred as a result of the use of the information contained within this document, including, but not limited to, errors, omissions, or inaccuracies.

Free Bonus from Silvia Hill available for limited time

Hi Spirituality Lovers!

My name is Silvia Hill, and first off, I want to THANK YOU for reading my book.

Now you have a chance to join my exclusive spirituality email list so you can get the ebooks below for free as well as the potential to get more spirituality ebooks for free! Simply click the link below to join.

P.S. Remember that it's 100% free to join the list.

~~$27~~ FREE BONUSES

- 9 Types of Spirit Guides and How to Connect to Them
- How to Develop Your Intuition: 7 Secrets for Psychic Development and Tarot Reading
- Tarot Reading Secrets for Love, Career, and General Messages

Access your free bonuses here
https://livetolearn.lpages.co/sun-signs-paperback/

Table of Contents

INTRODUCTION ... 1
CHAPTER 1: INTRODUCING ASTROLOGY ... 3
CHAPTER 2: PLANETS: THE SOURCE OF ENERGY ... 14
CHAPTER 3: ZODIAC SIGNS: THE TYPE OF ENERGY ... 26
CHAPTER 4: THE HOUSES: WHERE THE ENERGY MANIFESTS ... 38
CHAPTER 5: DISCOVERING YOUR SUN SIGN ... 46
CHAPTER 6: IDENTIFYING YOUR MOON SIGN ... 71
CHAPTER 7: SUN-MOON COMBINATIONS I - EARTH-SUN SIGNS ... 97
CHAPTER 8: SUN-MOON COMBINATIONS II: AIR SUN SIGNS ... 110
CHAPTER 9: SUN-MOON COMBINATIONS ILL: WATER SUN SIGNS ... 121
CHAPTER 10: SUN-MOON COMBINATIONS IV: FIRE SUN SIGNS ... 133
CONCLUSION ... 144
HERE'S ANOTHER BOOK BY SILVIA HILL THAT YOU MIGHT LIKE ... 146
FREE BONUS FROM SILVIA HILL AVAILABLE FOR LIMITED TIME ... 147
REFERENCES ... 148

Introduction

The stars can tell you who you are and who you are destined to be. The secrets behind this lie in your Sun sign. The Sun shines in the center of your natal chart, the map of celestial bodies at the time of your birth, influencing the energies of all other objects around it. Sun signs are studied by a specific branch of astrology that reveals your innermost desires, goals, instincts, beliefs, and what the universe may have in store for you in the future. It can help you understand why you think, feel, and behave in general or even in specific situations and why other people's personalities may differ when compared to yours.

You may be familiar with some basic astrological terms if you check your horoscope. However, by introducing you to a more specific astrological language, this book will help you discover your Sun sign more confidently. You will learn what the terms Sun signs and Moon signs refer to and how they are related to the zodiac. You will see how the Sun determines the standards you use to measure yourself and which you show to the outside world. You will also understand how the moon defines the marks you would like to leave behind, even if you are not aware of them yet.

Both the Sun and the Moon influence the main events of your life, and they guide you on your path to becoming the type of person their combination indicates you will be. You will also learn that your Sun sign is only the core of your personality. The other aspects of your natal chart, such as your zodiac sign, house placement, the phase of the moon, or the quality of the element ruling the season of your birth, outline your personality in finer detail.

Sun sign astrology can be a valuable tool to uncover the hidden strength you can use to persevere in life. You can think of your Sun sign as a vessel for all the different potential you can unearth. The opportunities you can reveal from a detailed study of your birth chart can be surprising. So, if you are ready to delve into the hidden depths of your personality, the only thing you have to do is keep reading this book. Although the Sun sign is just a piece of the larger whole, knowing what it holds for you can enormously impact your spiritual growth and happiness.

Chapter 1:
Introducing Astrology

If you have spent even a tiny bit of time on social media lately, you have probably encountered astrology. Memes about star signs and their effect on a person's personality are more popular than ever, and terms like Mercury retrograde and Mars retrograde have become part of daily conversation. In short, astrology is no longer the realm of older people and those who are out of touch. It has gone mainstream.

That said, if social media is your first real introduction to astrology, it can be enormously confusing to try and understand how it works. While most of us know our star signs, that information is almost everything we know on the topic. We may read our horoscopes, but we are unaware of how they were crafted and how other parts of our natal chart may affect our lives.

Before exploring astrology in detail, you first need to understand what astrology is. With a strong base knowledge of the subject, you will better understand the importance of your star sign and how the slightest changes in the skies can affect your life.

Understanding Astrology

According to Merriam-Webster, astrology is *"the divination of the supposed influences of the stars and planets on human affairs and terrestrial events by the positions and aspects."*

Pretty clear, right?

You are probably even more confused after reading that definition.

In essence, astrology studies celestial objects, like the stars and planets. Based on observations about their positions, astrology can make predictions about a person's life or how events in our lives and on earth will unfold.

It is essential to remember that astrology is not an exact science. Perfecting astrological analysis can take a lifetime, and even veteran, experienced astrologers learn more and refine their processes daily.

History of Astrology

This practice has a long history. Astrology can trace its origins to the 3rd millennium BC, and scholars today believe it developed along with calendar systems that were used to predict the changes in seasons. People would interpret the movement of celestial objects as communication from the gods and, for a period of time, astrology and astronomy were indistinguishable from one another.

Astrology spread far and wide from its origins in Mesopotamia, India, and China. Astrological systems in these countries are very different from the ones we know today in the West, and exploring Indian and Chinese astrology would need entire books dedicated to them.

However, in terms of astrology, as we know it today, you can trace back its roots to Egypt and Greece. One of the peoples who learned astrology from the Mesopotamians were the Persians, and, following their conquest of Egypt in 525 BC, they introduced the subject to their own lands. Following Alexander the Great's occupation of Egypt in 332 BC, the Egyptians, in turn, introduced the Greeks to astrology.

For a time, astrology took two different directions and developed differently in Ptolemaic Egypt and Greece. In Ptolemaic Egypt, three different forms of astrology, Mesopotamian, Babylonian, and native Egyptian, combined to produce the first type of horoscopic astrology. The horoscopes used by the Ptolemaic Egyptians were very different from horoscopes as we understand them today, but they formed the basis without which today's Western astrology would be completely different.

The Egyptian astrology.
See page for author, CC BY 4.0 <https://creativecommons.org/licenses/by/4.0>, via Wikimedia Commons:
https://commons.wikimedia.org/wiki/File:Astrology;_the_Egyptian_zodiac._Coloured_engraving_by_J._Cha_Wellcome_V0024917.jpg

The Greeks continuously explored new astrological concepts, including the newly developed horoscopic astrology. However, one of the most popular types of astrology was theurgic astrology, which was focused on helping a person's soul ascend to the stars and reach the gods.

Greek influence also helped spread astrology in Rome, especially following the Roman conquest of Greece. For a portion of time following the Roman conquest, astrology was relegated to a study with minor importance and only concerned the lower classes of society. Astrology was also significantly associated with Babylon.

Babylonia was known as Chaldea in Rome, and the link between the Babylonians and astrology was so deep that they used the term "Chaldean wisdom" to refer to any form of divination involving the planet and the stars.

Over time, astrology rose to prominence once more in Rome. The first references to astrology in Roman texts were from the writings of Cato and Juvenal in the 2nd century BC, both of whom caution against the divinatory powers of the "Chaldeans" and their astrologers. However, by the time of Augustus (who ruled from 27 BC to14 AD), astrology was used as a way to legitimize the emperor's right to rule. Augustus' stepson and heir, Tiberius, was the first emperor to have a court astrologer. The astrologer, Thrasyllus of Mendes, was also a personal friend of the emperor.

Most astrological texts from the Roman Empire were written in Greek, emphasizing the importance of the Greeks in the development of astrology. However, this also meant that following the downfall of the Western Roman Empire and the decline of the Greek language in Western Europe, astrology also declined in popularity once again.

While astrology was rising and falling in popularity under the Romans, it was also enormously popular in the Islamic world. This was the first time astrology and astronomy were differentiated, and Arabic astrology texts would become extremely popular in Europe.

These Arabic texts led to a resurgence of interest in the subject in Europe during the 10th century, and Greek and Roman theories were revived in the 12th and 13th centuries. By the 13th century, doctors had combined medicine with astrology, and by the 1500s, they were legally required to calculate the position of the moon before performing complex medical procedures like surgeries in some parts of Europe.

However, the differentiation of astrology and astronomy also meant a loss of interest in the subject from the scientific community. There was little scientific focus on it by the end of the 18th century.

Among the public, however, astrology has always ebbed and flowed. Popularity in the subject declined at the end of the Renaissance and has been up and down ever since. It would regain a strong following by the 1960s, a following that has continued to this day.

How Astrology Works

Astrologers study the connections between celestial activity and events on earth. These earthly events can affect one single person or society at large.

The events affected by the movement of celestial objects can be anything from your interpersonal relationships and career to your health or any aspect of your life. Astrologers who work with individuals will also create a birth (or natal) chart for those requiring one.

A birth chart is essentially a snapshot of what the sky looked like at the exact moment and location of your birth. The sky is divided into 12 sections or signs, and your birth chart not only allows astrologers to understand what positions the planets, Sun, and Moon were in when you were born but also a host of other information that allows them to make predictions.

Other astrologers only look at the signs under which you were born. These signs (the 12 zodiac signs) are based on the date of your birth, and astrologers look at the movement of planets and other bodies in and out of the section of the sky that "belongs" to your sign to make predictions and write horoscopes.

Astrologers also use your natal chart for other purposes, such as determining who you should marry, your compatibility with your current partner (based on both your natal charts), and much more. They can also use it to help you better understand your personality and path in life, as well as what your life focus should be.

Other parts of your birth chart include:

- **Houses:** There are 12 houses in each birth chart, each representing a different part of your life, such as relationships, career, etc. Your birth chart allows an astrologer to understand in which house each celestial body was placed at your birth.
- **Degrees:** This is the precise location of a planet. Its general location tells you which sign it is in, while the degree essentially serves as the planet's home address. Degrees are important when predicting transits and can help astrologers determine how a particular day, week, or month may affect

your chart.

- **Aspects:** A way to determine how planets and other celestial bodies interact with each other.

Other Aspects of Your Natal Chart

Natal charts, and astrology in general, are not strictly predictive. A natal chart reading, for example, can give you a better understanding of existing behavioral patterns, both the good and the bad.

This light into your life may feel uncomfortable, but after a few sessions with an astrologer, you will feel better and more connected with yourself. Additionally, it could also help spark healthy changes in your life, allowing you to develop a new personality without first having to go through the process of recognizing negative behavioral patterns.

Armed with your natal chart, an effective astrologer can tell you what goals your soul wants to achieve in its current lifetime, both in your career and otherwise. They can then help you interpret those goals. This is especially effective for people who are unsure of what path they want to take

You can also find other information, such as any trauma your soul has from a past life. Birth charts can also provide an insight into your family life, including your relationships with close family members such as parents and siblings (if you have any). It can give you a better understanding of any familial trauma you may be carrying and help you get started on resolving these issues.

Reading Birth Charts

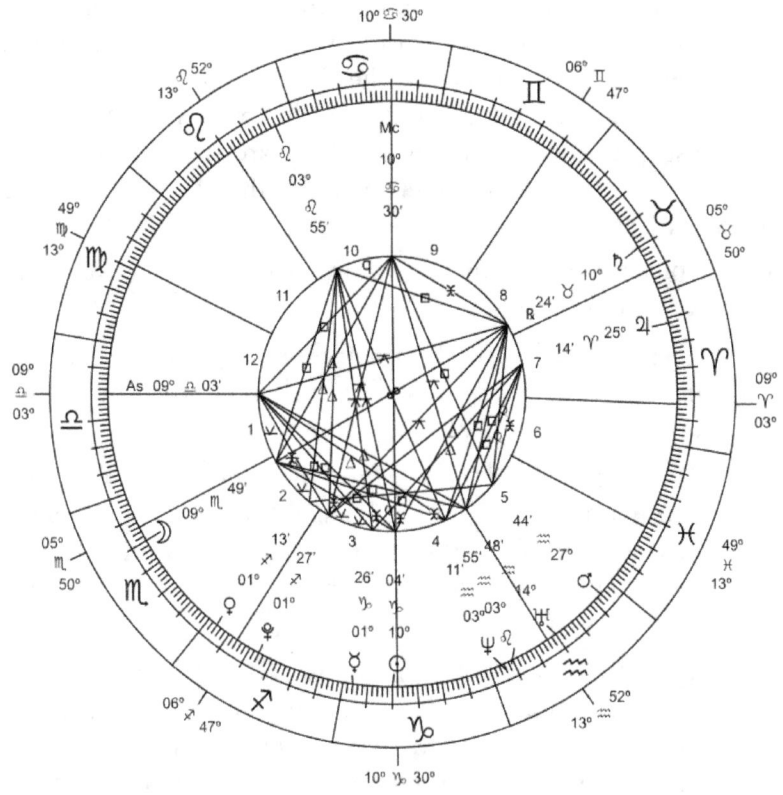

Sample birth chart.
Fred the Oyster, CC BY-SA 4.0 <https://creativecommons.org/licenses/by-sa/4.0>, via Wikimedia Commons: https://commons.wikimedia.org/wiki/File:Astrological_Chart_-_New_Millennium.svg

Originally, a person would have to be a trained astrologer to be able to effectively read your birth chart. Creating these natal charts requires a lot of math. This meant that you would have to confirm that your astrologer knew and understood math sufficiently before getting a natal chart reading.

However, modern-day readings could not be more different. As long as you know the exact time, date, and location of your birth, you can plug in this information to one of many similar websites online and receive a basic natal chart within seconds. While these charts do not give you near the level of detail professional charts do, they can often be a good starting point for people interested in the practice.

Additionally, these services often do not interpret or analyze your results. Instead, they either offer you a complete chart for you to interpret or a summary of the key points, including your ascendant and the location of the planets in your chart. While some services also provide interpretations, these are generally computer-generated and more generic interpretations than you would receive from a skilled astrologist.

If you plan to read your own chart, here are some key tips to help you with your analysis:

- **The Sun Sign:** Your Sun sign represents who you are at all times, regardless of what you are doing, who you are with, or how your life changes
- **The Moon Sign:** Your Moon sign represents the side of you that is more "hidden," a side that very few people are privy to, and the part of you that guides you when you feel lost. It plays an important part in your decision-making process.
- **The Ascendant Sign:** Your ascendant sign depends on which constellation was on your horizon at the exact moment of your birth. The ascendant sign changes far more frequently than the Sun or Moon signs – every hour or two, which is why astrologers place so much emphasis on knowing the exact hour of your birth. This sign (also known as your rising sign) represents how others see you, and it is usually the first part of yourself you show to new people.
- **Inner Planets:** The inner planets are Mercury, Venus, Mars, the Sun, and the Moon. Each of these planets carries a different meaning, but in general, these planets help you understand your core personality traits and your basic needs and desires. Mercury controls your communication style and your mind, Venus rules your romantic relationships, and Mars has sway over your actions and overall energy. Your core personality traits change depending on which signs these planets are in.

- **Outer Planets:** Jupiter, Saturn, Uranus, Neptune, and Pluto are the outer planets. They rule over more abstract aspects of your life. Jupiter rules over your luck and progress, Saturn over your self-discipline and your fears, Uranus over change in general, Neptune rules over your dreams and your healing ability, and Pluto over your power in general and transformative abilities.
- **Your Ruling Planet:** Your ruling planet is the planet associated with your ascendant sign. The planet's qualities give you insight into who you are, what things and attributes you value, and what motivation and principles rule your behavior. You are also more affected by the movements of your ruling planet than those of other planets. For example, if your ruling planet is Mercury, you will be more affected by Mercury retrograde than people with a different ruling planet.
- **The Midheaven Sign:** Some astrologers also focus on your midheaven sign. This sign is the highest point at the top of your chart and represents the southernmost high point above the horizon at the exact moment of your birth. Your midheaven sign allows you to better understand your career and life path. It helps you understand where you should aim to be in your life, what path you should follow, and what mark you are destined to leave through your achievements. It is, essentially, a representation of all your achievements as seen through other people's eyes, including the eyes of society, and can help you further explore your life goal.

Analyzing the intricate details of a natal chart can be challenging, especially if you have no previous experience. If you misinterpret a single movement, you could misinterpret your entire chart.

So, while getting overarching themes from a computer-generated natal chart is possible, it is always best to see a professional if you want a proper reading. They will better help you understand the intricate movement of the stars and how they affect your life on earth.

So, Why Astrology?

Now that you have a better understanding of astrology, the next question many people ask is, "Why should I care?" While astrology is popular, belief in it is certainly not universal, and many people do not understand how a natal chart or the daily horoscope can help them.

For people who believe in astrology, its value lies in the predictions it can offer about a person's life. While you may not be able to change everything that an astrologer predicts, knowing it is coming will allow you to better prepare and anticipate the effects.

However, even if you are on the fence about your belief in astrology, exploring it further on your own or with a trained astrologist can benefit you.

Studies have shown that astrology can encourage self-reflection in individuals, helping them to better understand themselves and the world around them. Additionally, astrology offers people a chance to make sense of the world's chaos, giving them a sense of control they may have otherwise lacked. It can help them deal with negative life events and uncertainty.

People are particularly drawn to astrology during tumultuous times in their personal lives and the world around them. For example, astrology found greater popularity in the United States during the Great Depression and in Germany in the years between the two world wars. The insight astrology provides you with deals with the realities of life better, which is why people turn to it in challenging periods during their lives.

Additionally, many people find it hard to cope with a sense of ambiguity and uncertainty, especially when making plans for the future. Astrological predictions help give you the knowledge and information you need to make informed decisions for yourself and the people around you.

As we have discussed in this chapter, one of the most important parts of astrology is your Sun sign. While you probably already know your Sun sign, you have also likely realized that there is more to it than simply your daily or weekly horoscope. Now that you understand the importance of astrology and how Sun signs play into astrology, this book will help you explore the impact your sign can have on your life.

In the next chapter, you will learn more about the effect of the planets on your life and their function as a source of energy. It will help you to understand how astrologers use the placement of the planets to make predictions about you, the world, and other people.

We will then explore the zodiac signs in further detail, including their elements, qualities, personality, and positive and negative traits. Following this, we will explore the 12 houses, what zodiac signs they are ruled by, and what aspects of your life they represent and rule.

Next, we will move on to helping you discover your Sun and Moon signs. The Sun-Moon combination of your signs can help you to better understand your personality than those individual signs. We will also look at the Sun-Moon combinations according to their respective elements. We'll cover all four elements: earth, air, water, and fire.

By the time you finish reading this book, you will have a good understanding of your Sun and Moon signs and how they affect your life. This will help you better understand any horoscopes you consult in the future and give you the knowledge needed to help you shape your life going forward.

So, what are you waiting for? All that is left now is to turn the page to the next chapter and continue reading!

Chapter 2:
Planets: The Source of Energy

As you have learned from the previous chapter, planets have played an enormous role in astrological predictions since the practice began. Each heavenly body is a key to birth charts in astrology because their energy is associated with intrinsic human characteristics and values. While each astrological planet has its own energy source, they are also influenced by other entities in the solar system. Depending on their interaction, their combined force affects people's behavior differently. This chapter discusses how astrology uses planet placements, movements, and qualities to provide predictions and insights into the world and the human psyche. By learning the characteristic energies and glyphs linked to each planet, you can learn how they affect your natal chart and how you can determine their influence.

Astrological Planets and Birth Charts

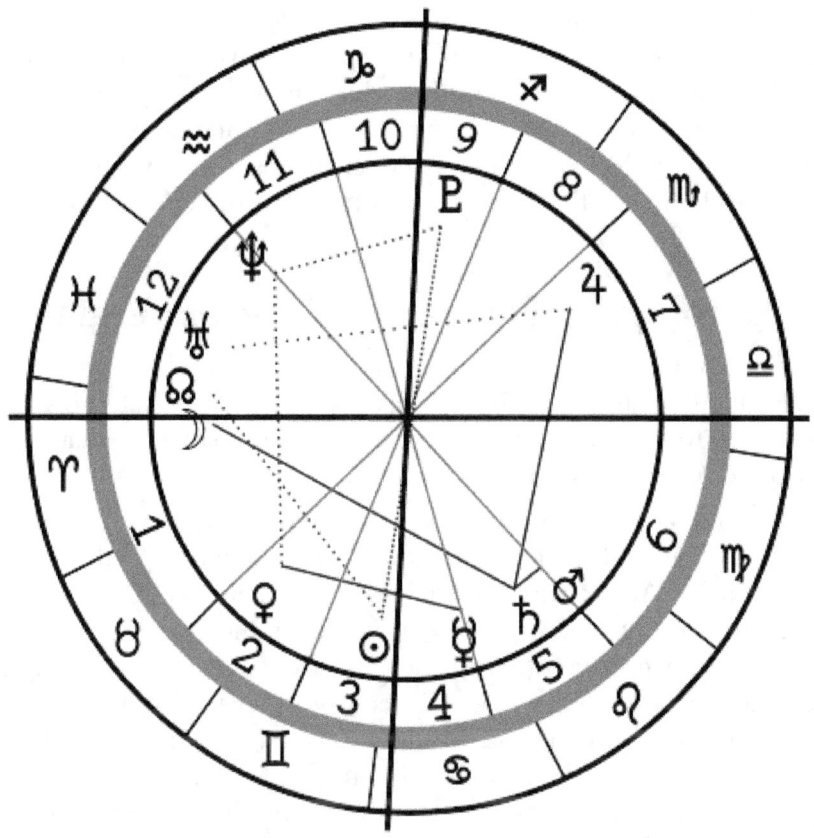

Sample birth chart with signs and planet glyphs.
Rursus, CC BY-SA 3.0 <https://creativecommons.org/licenses/by-sa/3.0>, via Wikimedia Commons: https://commons.wikimedia.org/wiki/File:Birth_chart.svg

The astrological planets rule over zodiac signs and are located in one of the 12 zodiac houses. Your birth chart is a complex trove of information that reveals the precise location of each heavenly body and zodiac sign when you entered this world. From that time on, they will have influenced you. Depending on their location at the time you were born, each planet has a different impact on your life. In ancient astrology, the planets themselves were seen as representations of characteristics people may display throughout the course of their lives. Today, we know that not only do planets determine human traits, but they also affect different areas of our lives, determining how they will play out. By drawing from this symbolism, you can peek into any aspect of your life, from health to relationships to professional development.

It is important to note that the astrological planets are not represented similarly on all birth charts. Some will show the planets displayed in the same constellation while, in others, they are located at greater distances from another. For a more precise reading, it is recommended to go with a natal chart that displays the exact distance between the planets, as this can be crucial to their astrological function.

Astrological Planets and Their Energies

Before you can learn how to make or read a birth chart, you must understand the basic meaning of each astrological planet. This will allow you to interpret their positioning in your chart and what their movements can bring you in the future.

The Sun and the Moon, the two astrological bodies visible to the naked eye most of the time, were the most studied heavenly bodies for centuries. And to this day, we know that their energies affect our lives the most. However, as soon as astronomers and astrologers began observing the other planets in the solar system, it soon became evident that these objects can also influence our characteristics and behavior. At first, people were only aware of the effects of Mercury, Venus, Mars, Jupiter, and Saturn, as the rest of the planets were considered to be too far from the Sun. Nowadays, we know that Uranus, Neptune, and even Pluto can influence our lives depending on their position and movement.

Here is an overview of all the heavenly bodies, including their placements and energies in life and within yourself.

Sun

Keywords: Primal personality, ego, stamina, consciousness, vitality

Glyph as Seen on One's Birth Chart: ☉ - Shield with a circle inside it

Placement in the Solar System: Center, providing energy to all the planets and celestial bodies

Time to Transit between Signs: 1 month

What It Represents within You: Your ego, vital energy, and the core of your personality.

What It Represents in Life: Collective focus, community energy, and strength

While it is considered to be a star – not a planet – in astrology and birth charts, the Sun is the most important object in them. Why? Because this luminary object determines the positions of all other planets and zodiac signs at any given time, determining the birth signs of every individual person. Its impact is so broad that it can influence entire communities and nations, independently of the characteristics of individual members.

When it comes to your own personality, the Sun is what determines what comes after the phrase "I am." It brings out your *core personality*, which is determined by the location of the Sun in the sky at the time you came into this world. This planet will also influence how you express your creativity and how you use your vital life force. Since the Sun transits into another sign each month, you can get more precise information about your personality.

Moon

Keywords: Emotions, mood, unconsciousness, desires, instincts, and habits

Glyph as Seen on One's Birth Chart: ☽/☾ - A crescent from either side

Placement in the Solar System: Between Venus and Mars, close to the earth

Time to Transit between Signs: 2-3 days

What It Represents within You: Your soul and inner desires

What It Represents in Life: Collective inner power of all humans beings

Like the Sun, the moon is not a planet in astronomy, and it has far less impact on the movement of other planets. However, according to astrology, the moon has just as much influence as other celestial bodies on your birth and life cycle. Its close proximity to earth provides us with a unique source of emotional power, lending entire communities confidence to rise and overcome difficulties.

Interestingly enough, the position of the moon at the time you were born can bring forward characteristics that are vastly different from the ones provided by the location of the Sun at the same time. Since it focuses more on your feelings and intrinsic senses, this planet is more likely to show you who you *want to be* rather than *who you think you are*. It can also reveal how to best nurture your emotions to get what you desire. To learn all of this, you must uncover the exact location of the moon on your natal chart, as the transit time of 2-3 days can make a vast difference in your fate.

Mercury

Keywords: Communication, rational thinking, intellect, language skills, and natural intelligence

Glyph as Seen on One's Birth Chart: ☿ The head and the winged cap of Mercury

Placement in the Solar System: Closest planet to the Sun, absorbing the most energy of all planets

Time to Transit between Signs: 3-4 weeks

What It Represents within You: Your rational mind and natural communication style

What It Represents in Life: Mental power of a community and the effects of the media and global economy

Mercury is the planet responsible for communication - or the lack of it. On the one hand, the strong influence of this planet comes from its energy, which is the closest planet to the Sun. The other reason Mercury affects human lives is that it is the second closest planet to earth. Its quick transit period means that it can cause quick mood shifts in entire communities, bringing the members closer to each other or pushing them apart.

The energy of Mercury can determine how you receive, process, analyze and transmit information about your environment. Mercury can affect everything from daily routines to communication in complicated long-term relationships. It can also counteract the emotional influence of the moon, allowing you to process everything through rational thinking. While often encouraging you to explore complex ideas, Mercury will also prompt you to think them through entirely. Since the planet transits every 3-4 weeks, knowing its precise location is needed if you want to uncover how it affects you.

Venus

Keywords: Love, emotional attachment, relationships, beauty, art, and harmony

Time to Transit between Signs: 4-5 weeks

Glyph as Seen on One's Birth Chart: ♀ - The female symbol

Placement in the Solar System: The second closest to the Sun, located between Mercury and Earth

What It Represents within You: Your language and romantic and aesthetic preferences

What It Represents in Life: The emotional energy of a community and the sense of connection between all members

Even though it is often viewed only as the planet of love, Venus has much more influence in people's lives than just facilitating romantic relationships. Its energy is known to resolve conflicts by prompting people to display empathy, compassion, and social grace instead of disdain or fear, even toward those they do not know. Venus encourages the masses to seek out different types of relationships, which is how communities are formed. It brings harmony whenever and wherever it is needed.

Venus also affects our ability to manage our finances, although this varies depending on individual values. Depending on its location at the time of your birth, Venus will provide you with different core values. And everything you do in your finances and relationships must align with these values. Venus is often used in love-match comparisons as it can tell you how a person wants to be loved. A match can also come out in art and sense of style, especially in friendships and other types of non-romantic relationships.

Mars

Keywords: Need for action, aggression, sex, desire, passion, competition, and courage

Time to Transit between Signs: 6-7 weeks

Glyph as Seen on One's Birth Chart: ♂ - The male symbol

Placement in the Solar System: Fourth planet from the Sun, located between Earth and Jupiter

What It Represents within You: Your passion, determination, and sex drive

What It Represents in Life: Collective focus and levels of high passion and aggression

Being the closest planet to the Earth, Mars has an incredibly powerful hold on our physical energy. Often called masculine energy, the physical drive of Mars provides different levels of endurance and encourages people to act, even when they feel unable to do so. However, this may often come out as aggression and willingness to cause conflicts, leading to community distress. This planet also rules passion and sexuality, acting as a complementary tool to the emotional connections developed with the help of Venus.

Depending on its position on your birth chart, Mars can offer some insight into what physical activity will work best for your body. For some people, this planet only provides low levels of physical energy, so they are only able to engage in passive exercise. Others are blessed with the ability to take up intense activities or even choose the intensity they want to engage in. While typically a great motivator, when in retrograde, Mars can cause even people willing to take action to step back and wait.

Jupiter

Keywords: Luck, optimism, growth, abundance, expansion, and understanding

Time to Transit between Signs: 12-13 Months

Glyph as Seen on One's Birth Chart: ♃ - A hieroglyph of an eagle

Placement in the Solar System: The fifth planet from the Sun, located between Mars and Saturn

What It Represents within You: Where you will find your true luck

What It Represents in Life: Collective sense of hope, empowerment, and growth

Since it is the largest planet in our solar system, Jupiter was the first one discovered after the Sun and the Moon. This probably explains why it has so many influential roles, including the ones in religious beliefs and faiths, philosophy, and even luck. Jupiter has excited people about their fate and helped them accept it for centuries. Depending on its location on one's birth chart, people believed, and still believe, that it can bring luck.

Jupiter's energy can make you want to seek out and explore new adventures with joy, passion, and enthusiasm. Even though this planet may push you out of your comfort zone, it will only be to show your new horizons. It shows you that you can experience all this in many forms as long as they keep you happy and help you grow. Remember that the luck and abundance it promises on your natal chart may come in a different form than you would expect it to arrive.

Saturn

Keywords: Law, structure, discipline, restriction, responsibility, ambition, and obligation

Time to Transit between Signs: 2-3 Years

Glyph as Seen on One's Birth Chart: ♄ - An ancient representation of a sickle or scythe

Placement in the Solar System: The sixth planet from the Sun, located between Jupiter and Uranus

What It Represents within You: The place where your responsibility lies and the life lessons you learn

What It Represents in Life: Global structures, inducing community, governments, and collective karma

Saturn also has a long-term effect on people's lives, often showing up in stages to show the path one is meant to take. It often guides younger community members, particularly when they become young adults ready to contribute to society. If Saturn returns at this time, it will guide the youngsters through a series of tasks they must complete to find their identity and purpose in life.

As an individual, Saturn will help you through all the milestones of your life, ensuring that you learn the responsibilities that come with your life's purpose. It will encourage you to keep up the hard work and work towards your goals. Depending on which house the planet was in when you were born, you may thrive on structure. This will also allow you to view each challenging task as an opportunity to grow instead of an obstacle.

Uranus

Keywords: Unpredictable changes, reformation, eccentricity, rebellion, newness

Time to Transit between Signs: 7 Years

Glyph as Seen on One's Birth Chart: ⛢ - Combined signs symbolizing the Sun and the spear of Mars

Placement in the Solar System: The seventh planet from the Sun, located between Saturn and Neptune

What It Represents within You: Your eccentric side and how you express it

What It Represents in Life: Science, progressive and future-oriented communal growth, technology, digital communication

Uranus is often called the modern planet, not just because its impact on human societies has been discovered long after the first six planets. Nothing can provide people with more inspiring energy than Uranus. In fact, its effects on human evolution and advancements have been so great that it even surprised astrologists. The planet prompts generation after generation to develop numerous innovations in science and technology. Although this often means breaking the rules, as history has shown, this can sometimes be more beneficial for the common good than anyone has thought.

Regarding individual characteristics, Uranus is responsible for eccentricities, unexplained need for change and liberation, and even rebellion. Depending on which zodiac house the planet was in when you were born, Uranus will either lend you the energy to fight against injustice or move past it in a totally unexpected, innovative way. The energy of this planet will encourage you to express your individuality in various degrees and forms, including in the form of art, technology, and science.

Neptune

Keywords: Intuition, dreams, mysticism, visions, delusion, imagination,

Time to Transit between Signs: 10-12 Years

Glyph as Seen on One's Birth Chart: ♆ - The trident of Neptune

Placement in the Solar System: The eighth planet from the Sun, located between Uranus and Pluto

What It Represents within You: Your dreams, imagination, and your creative and mystical side

What It Represents in Life: Global artistic interests, community outrage, spirituality, religion, and illusions

As the second to last astrological planet in our solar system,

Neptune is linked to slow and mystical influences. It inspires different generations with different dreams, visions, and illusions. Neptune can also determine people's values and ideals, equipping them with different degrees of the ability to see the truth. This is particularly true if the planet shifts into retrograde, which sometimes undoes the effects of the previous illusion.

Depending on its location at the time of your birth, it may encourage you to only accept the truth from yourself and from those around you. That being said, the most beneficial effects of this planet come from the sense of oneness with the universe it can provide. Remember, Neptune can be tricky; just as it can lend you its energy for psychic influences, it can also hide the truth from you.

Pluto

Keywords: Power, evolution, transformation, death, and rebirth

Time to Transit between Signs: 12-15 Years

Glyph as Seen on One's Birth Chart: ♇, - A monogram made from the letters P and L or a bident with an orb

Placement in the Solar System: Located after Neptune, the farthest planet from the Sun

What It Represents within You: Your ability to transform your life and your soul's rebirth

What It Represents in Life: Global sources of power, including financial institutions, and governments

Even though Pluto lost its status as a planet in astronomy, in astrology, its place as one of the most influential celestial bodies remains the same. Due to its slow transit time and location in the solar system, Pluto's effects are much subtler. Yet, they can be equally profound, especially as they are mostly known for their transformative qualities. Its energy allows communities to thrive and empower themselves through different institutions, which may or may not be for the common good.

While the effects of the moon can come with darker psychological aspects for the masses, this is rarely the case for individuals. Pluto can lend you varying amounts of regenerative powers depending on its location at the time of your birth. So, if you notice that your life is not heading in the direction you wanted it to, you can transform into a better version of yourself by letting go of the past and looking toward the future.

Chapter 3: Zodiac Signs: The Type of Energy

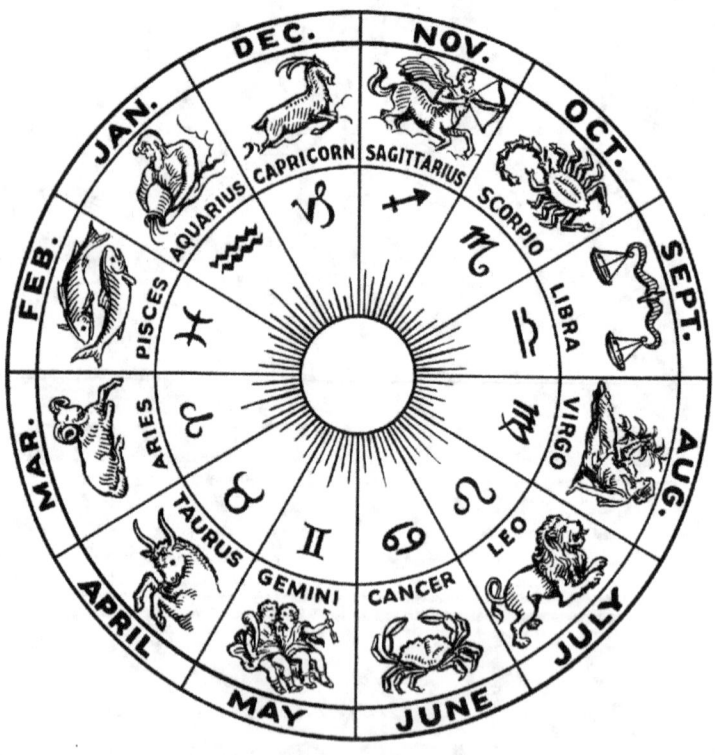

Zodiac Symbols.
https://commons.wikimedia.org/wiki/File:Zodiac_(PSF).png

While astrological planets are known to be a powerful source of energy, the zodiac signs represent a different type of power. And the reason you need to consider this when examining your natal chart is twofold. For one, zodiac energy is subtler than that of your ruling planet. While planets can determine your core personality, the rest of your traits come from the energy of the zodiac signs and houses. Second, the planets move through the zodiac signs, mixing their energies with the signs and creating combinations that give unique qualities to each individual person. In addition, each sign has a ruling planet which influences its overall energy output. This energy, albeit not as strong as the planets, can vary greatly depending on whether the sign is under the influence of its ruling planet or another one near it at any given moment. This chapter will teach you about the associations of each zodiac sign and how their energy influences people's lives.

Zodiac Sign Associations and Qualities

Before delving into the specific energies of each zodiac sign, you need to learn a little more about their association with the four cardinal elements. Apart from being ruled over planets and the power of their houses, each zodiac sign is influenced by one of the four elements of nature, Air, Earth, Fire, and Water. These elements give each zodiac sign different qualities, determining the undertone of personality traits. However, not only do the four elements represent a distinctive quality, but within each of them, there are also unique nuances called quadruplicities. They are three unique qualities within each element:

- **Mutable:** The most *adaptable* quality, allowing the signs that possess it to persevere in any situation. However, it can also make them indecisive even in situations when time is of the essence or if their future depends on making a definite decision.
- **Cardinal:** The signs with a cardinal trait are open-minded and always ready to think about the bigger picture. Unfortunately, they will not always follow through with all the magnificent ideas they come up with when they brainstorm about a crucial aspect of life.

- **Fixed:** The most dependable and strong-willed signs; these are not afraid to face any challenge. Their stubbornness to overcome will occasionally place them in uncharted territories they are not equipped to explore.

Each of these qualities can be found in each element, and their combination will create distinct personality traits in the different zodiac signs. Below, you will see which sign is associated with which elements and which quality of the said element.

Aries

Nickname: The "I am" sign

Zodiac Symbol: ♈- The ram

Birth Month: March 21 - April 19

Element: Fire

Quality: Cardinal

As a cardinal fire sign, Aries is known for being dynamic, competitive, impulsive, and fearless, all of which come from the sign's active and masculine archetype. They have an insatiable appetite for conquering new goals, whether winning a prize or acquiring a new skill. And the higher the stakes for this new goal, the better for the Aries. They also focus on communicating their beliefs to the outside world, which makes them great leaders. Aries knows how to adapt and innovate. They also have a way of getting others to follow their lead by enticing fierce competition.

Positive Traits: Aries is always ready to take action, even if this means overcoming a limiting belief or fear. People born under this sign do not hold grudges and will always let you know where you stand with them. Aries can be great athletes as they always focus on their performance.

Negative Traits: Since Aries prefers to act according to their own beliefs, they are not keen to listen to advice and will even avoid conversations for this reason. When they communicate, they tend to be direct, which is often conceived as cruel and insensitive.

Taurus

Nickname: The "I have" sign

Zodiac Symbol: ♉ - The bull

Birth Month: April 20 - May 20

Element: Earth

Quality: Fixed

The fixed quality of this earth sign makes it the most resolute and grounded of all the zodiac signs. Not only is Taurus keen on standing their ground, but they will do it so stubbornly that most people find it easier to just go along with them. And they will definitely take their time with everything. Despite this, the archetype of the Taurus personality is peaceful and indulgent. As long as no one bothers them when they are working on their own goal, they will be happy to share the fruits of their hard labor. They will enjoy it themselves too, along with any luxury they can get their hands on!

Positive Traits: Patience is a virtue that Taurus holds in high esteem. When faced with difficulties, they are resourceful and receptive. Taurus are skilled at arts and crafts and have the know-how to appreciate other creators' work too.

Negative Traits: Their peaceful nature often makes Taurus seem too complacent, even in situations that clearly are not working in their favor. They can be so fixated on their own creations that they will not even notice when they are being taken advantage of.

Gemini

Nickname: The "I think" sign

Zodiac Symbol: ♊ - The twins

Birth Month: May 21 - June 20

Element: Air

Quality: Mutable

As a mutable air sign, Gemini is the living embodiment of the famous "mercurial" quality. They use their witty and lighthearted nature to charm everyone around them. This is great because they can choose with whom to share a good talk and who will be the perfect company for a quiet moment, both of which they enjoy from time to time. Gemini is always keen to explore new ideas, which allows them to adapt to any circumstances and make the necessary changes to better their lives and the lives of those around them.

Positive Traits: The primary strength of Gemini lies in their intelligent and curious nature. Gemini will make the best of whatever situation they find themselves in. Their playful disposition allows them to easily establish communication with everyone they meet.

Negative Traits: Gemini's ability to jump from one interest to another can make people think that they will never know which "twin" they will be dealing with on any given day. This may earn them the reputation of being untrustworthy and emotionally distant.

Cancer

Nickname: The "I feel" sign

Zodiac Symbol: ♋ The crab

Birth Month: June 21 - July 22

Element: Water

Quality: Cardinal

Cancer is a cardinal water sign, which means they have a nurturing, compassionate and sentimental nature. The moon also influences their personality, which helps them dream about how to create the perfect home for their family. They may also represent a strong, supportive presence for their community. That said, Cancer typically prioritizes their relationships with their loved ones instead of creating new ones. They will give them everything that is in their power, and sometimes even more. If this happens, they will retreat for a bit of self-care so they can be up and ready to help others as soon as possible.

Positive Traits: Cancer has a kind and giving nature and is always ready to show emphasis and care for others. While they want to share what they can, they will not overwhelm you with unwanted advice or even their presence but will wait for you to become comfortable with them.

Negative Traits: Cancer can become so emotionally involved with their environment that it is hard for them to let go and make changes when needed. They may also project their willingness to help others, which can result in unhealthy, co-dependent relationships.

Leo

Nickname: The "I will" sign

Zodiac Symbol: ♌ - The lion

Birth Month: July 23 - August 22

Element: Fire

Quality: Fixed

Leo is typically confident, optimistic, generous, and cheerful as a fixed fire sign. Their charismatic nature makes it easy for them to connect with those around them, and this is only one of the things that they can accomplish, whatever their aim in life is. The other reason is that they will always prefer to take action instead of waiting for a solution. Even though they believe in luck, they have more confidence in achieving their goals. Their radiant energy is contagious, often inspiring their followers to change their own lives.

Positive Traits: Leo is a natural-born leader whose primary strength lies in their confidence. They are also always optimistic and will always find things they can be happy about. Not only do they lead with courage, but they are also very generous to those who rely on them.

Negative Traits: Being fixated on their own opinions often gets Leo in trouble, as they often have issues admitting they are wrong. Their tendency to steal the limelight may also make them seem ruthless and power-hungry. That can even lead them to forget those who helped them along their path to success.

Virgo

Virgo symbol.
Google, Apache License 2.0 <http://www.apache.org/licenses/LICENSE-2.0>, via Wikimedia Commons: https://commons.wikimedia.org/wiki/File:Green_Virgo_emoji.svg

Nickname: The "I analyze" sign

Zodiac Symbol: ♍ - The virgin

Birth Month: August 23 - September 22

Element: Earth

Quality: Mutable

Despite being an earth sign, the mutable quality of Virgo pushes their mind to work on several different frequencies at all times. Virgo loves to research whatever project they might be interested in and work hard for their goals. This goal is often helping others, like securing finances or meeting health needs. Virgo thrives on serving their nearest and dearest and will always make sure they know who to turn to with their problems. They are also detail-orientated and will keep all the information they gather neatly organized.

Positive Traits: Virgo is gifted with an incredible skill of adaptability, which, combined with their meticulous nature, makes them quick learners. They can decide what is useful and what is not at a moment's notice. However, instead of taking full advantage of it for themselves, they pride themselves on using this skill to help others.

Negative Traits: The highly functional mind of a Virgo can easily become overwrought with worries, which may or may not only exist only in their minds. They also tend to over-identify when their help is needed and can become overprotective of their loved ones.

Libra

Nickname: The "I relate" sign

Zodiac Symbol: ♎ - The scales

Birth Month: September 23 - October 22

Element: Air

Quality: Cardinal

As the cardinal air sign, Libras were born to bring justice, peace, and happiness into the lives of others. They appreciate beautiful art and being surrounded by like-minded people. While they prioritize bonds with particular individuals, this is never to their own benefit. Whether it is a working relationship, romantic relationship, or friendship, they will do everything to keep the other person happy. They will also stand up for what they believe in, especially if it benefits their loved ones. Libras tend to have romantic dreams, which they are not afraid to follow.

Positive Traits: Libras are great communicators and listeners and always try to see things from everyone else's perspective. They can put others first and care for others' well-being before they think of their own. Libras rarely get angry and give plenty of opportunities to those who wronged them to redeem themselves.

Negative Traits: Libras often cannot focus on their own goals because they are distracted by everyone else's problems. To keep the peace, they can compromise their values but will resent this later.

Scorpio

Nickname: The "I transform" sign

Zodiac Symbol: ♏ - The scorpion

Birth Month: October 23 - November 21

Element: Water

Quality: Fixed

This mysterious water sign is known for valuing their privacy above anything else in life. They seek power and are willing to work hard for it but rarely reveal their true motives to others. Scorpions demand attention not because they speak loudly but because they listen and take their time to get to know you. People are often drawn to their magnetic presence. They often seek solitude for spiritual purposes, as it gives them time and space to ponder. They may even turn from people they have a close emotional bond with if pressed too hard on personal matters.

Positive Traits: Whether they are committed to art, studies, or anything else, Scorpions are hard workers. They are also receptive and patient and are keen to learn the dynamics of any relationship by simply letting others speak or act first.

Negative Traits: Those born under this sign are slow to trust and have trouble revealing their weaknesses or asking for help. Despite this, they expect others to show the same intense emotions they feel but hide or show very little of them.

Sagittarius

Nickname: The "I see" sign

Zodiac Symbol: ♐ - The archer

Birth Month: November 22 - December 21

Element: Fire

Quality: Mutable

The free-spirited Sagittarius is always ready to seek a new adventure, although they rarely do this when in the company of other people. However, they like to socialize if they stay in one place long enough. In these times, they will be the life of the party, entertaining everyone with unfiltered tales about their latest adventure or philosophical discoveries. They are passionate about their beliefs and want to share them with everyone else before they change. Because as a mutable sign, Sagittarius is born to change constantly and will unconsciously seek this change.

Positive Traits: They are bold and optimistic and will let you see the brighter side of life in any situation. Their belief that everything will work out eventually gets rewarded with their adventure taking them to a place they are happy to explore. They are also fiercely independent and not afraid to tell you if they have a problem with someone invading their privacy.

Negative Traits: Due to their adventurous spirit, they are known to be non-committal. If they feel like it, they will not hesitate to make last-minute changes in their plans, even if this means breaking commitments with others.

Capricorn

Nickname: The "I use" sign

Zodiac Symbol: ♑ - The sea goat

Birth Month: December 22 - January 19

Element: Earth

Quality: Cardinal

As a cardinal earth sign, Capricorn is always motivated to achieve its goals. Despite being down-to-earth and traditional in many ways, Capricorns pride themselves on setting as many tasks for themselves as possible. If needed, they will employ industrious methods to persevere and will never stop their diligent work until they do. Although they tend to avoid large gatherings when accompanied by people they trust and enjoy being with, Capricorns exhibit a dry and often dark sense of humor. They can also show you the benefits of taking a pragmatic but proactive approach to any challenge.

Positive Traits: Capricorns are good judges of characters and will render a fair verdict if asked to rule in a dispute. They are also remarkably cool-headed and will always survey all the possibilities before deciding the proper way to pursue a goal.

Negative Traits: Capricorns tend to hold everyone around them to the same work ethic they possess, often leading to conflicts. They can even cease contact with people who fail to live up to these standards or are unwilling to put up with their grueling pace.

Aquarius

Aquarius symbol.
Google, Apache License 2.0 <http://www.apache.org/licenses/LICENSE-2.0>, via Wikimedia Commons: https://commons.wikimedia.org/wiki/File:Green_Aquarius_emoji.svg

Nickname: The "I know" sign

Zodiac Symbol: ♒ - The water-bearer

Birth Month: January 20 - February 18

Element: Air

Quality: Fixed

The ever-cool Aquarius stays true to its name and its fixed air quality. While they seem eccentric, people born under this sign are only in pursuit of their own individualistic ideals and beliefs. They believe in progress and are willing to help others, but their social life is somewhat superficial. They cultivate many relationships but will avoid deep and intimate connections. It is not uncommon for Aquarius to gravitate towards non-traditional arrangements, whether in work or private life. They find conventions boring and one-dimensional, so they will avoid them at all costs.

Positive Traits: The primary strengths of Aquarius lies in their intelligence and ability to find a fresh perspective. After examining a problem, they will always be able to come up with innovative solutions, which allows them to adapt to any circumstances.

Negative Traits: Their love for the complex forces them to view life as nothing more than a puzzle to be solved. Their abstract ideas can be hard to relate to. They use humor to deflect feelings or make others feel inferior when they feel attacked.

Pisces

Nickname: The "I believe" sign
Zodiac Symbol: ♓ - Two fishes
Birth Month: February 19 - March 20
Element: Air
Quality: Mutable

As a mutable air sign, Pisces is not only tuned in to their own emotions but is also empathetic to the feelings of others. They have the ability to heal emotional wounds and can speak up when someone needs counseling. Despite their high level of inner awareness, they find it easier to express their emotions through art than through regular speech. They often have a dreamy and romantic quality to them which comes from their keen sense of imagination and tendency to seek out spiritual explorations. They enjoy contemplating life and finding out how to adapt to new circumstances.

Positive Traits: Pisces is sympathetic and receptive to other people's feelings and ideas. They are always ready to offer helpful spiritual advice and as much of themselves in any relationship as possible. They can retain an air of innocence, no matter how many challenges they may face in life.

Negative Traits: Pisces take comments to heart and are easily emotionally wounded, especially regarding their art. Their selfless nature makes them needy and vulnerable to co-dependent relationships and toxic energies emanating from their environment.

Chapter 4: The Houses: Where the Energy Manifests

Anyone interested in learning a bit more about astrology will immediately come across the concept of the houses, and it can be quite difficult to understand in the beginning. However, if you have made a habit of checking your daily horoscope, then that is the start of delving deeper into astrology and all of the incredible details the practice entails. Astrology combines the study of many different disciplines, from astronomy to history, and getting to know the houses allows for a deeper appreciation for this much-maligned yet sophisticated art form. In addition to the planets and the signs themselves, the houses are an integral part of the moving elements behind the creation of birth charts. So, what are houses? This chapter will clear up some common misconceptions and will introduce you to the heart of not only astrology but where most metaphysical energies in this world manifest.

What Is a House?

Let us start from the very beginning and explain precisely what the concept of a house means in astrology. Basically, there are twelve ecliptic planes in astrology that divide up time and place as soon as someone is born. From there, their unique energies manifest, informing every other element that makes up the personality and destiny of an individual. If you look at a birth chart, you will find that each house is numbered counter-clockwise from the point of the first house. Also, they tend to be laid out in a very particular way in one's birth chart, with each house presiding over various aspects of one's life, including things like major relationship milestones, financial quandaries, and so on. Therefore, they are crucial to help us to better understand what may come later in our lives. Think of it this way. The houses form a vital part of your birth chart, which should be treated as a map of your life that can offer guidance if you choose to use it.

Houses and Symbols

The planets were aligned in different houses and signs when you were born. When you take the time to outline a birth chart yourself or go to an astrologer, they will take the time to interpret its meaning. That involves deciphering each planet's role and the house within that sign and mapping any obstacles or moments of good fortune that will happen to you. On every rotation, the planets will visit any of the twelve houses, lighting up different parts of your birth chart, which in turn energizes particular characteristics of the house. Astrologers tend to use twelve houses to predict several areas in your life that will come into focus, which could allow you to take the best possible action.

The birth chart is, of course, circular in nature. If you were to draw a circle and move clockwise, the first house could be found at what is noted as nine o'clock. This first house is often referred to as the cusp of the "beginning border," and as you move throughout the zodiac wheel, you will do so in a counter-clockwise direction. This movement is meant to represent the soul's evolution from the personal, the first house, to the greater society, the twelfth house.

Personal Houses

So, now you know that the houses on a birth chart are meant to track one's evolution as an individual to their rightful place in a collective. We can now break this down further and study the first six houses, which are referred to as *personal houses.*

Personal houses dominate our private and immediate lives. They cover our personal journeys, our environments, and our relationships with siblings, peers, and parents. In essence, they define our own particular expressions of who we are. An interpretation of someone whose chart possesses several planets in the first six houses is that they may have trouble leaving the nest, for example. Or, they may be inordinately attached to their childhood friendships, unable to make new connections as adults since nostalgia rules their thoughts. This is just one way in which seeing the houses in your charts may be able to tell you more about yourself, which is a dynamic that will be explored further in this chapter.

- **The First House**

The First House is often referred to as the House of the Self. Its cusp is the home of the Ascendant, the sign that resides on the eastern horizon at the exact moment of your birth. It lays the foundations for how you can define yourself as a person and who you will become. It also speaks to the individual's realization of their ultimate potential. The First House is ruled by the star sign Aries and the planet Mars.

This particular house rules early childhood. Everything from your first attempts at walking to your emergent worldview, regardless of how childlike and unformed, is considered to reside here. It answers key questions on how your personality will develop and the different elements that will inevitably shape your life. To sum up, the first house speaks to the parts of your personhood that are currently in existence and will solidify later.

- **The Second House**

The Second House is referred to as the House of Possessions. Of course, it alludes to what we actually own, although it is not limited to material possessions. It also refers to less tangible things we own, such as our feelings, our unique capabilities, and needs and wants. So, when someone tells you to "own up to it," in terms of astrology, you are presenting ownership over the Second House and all that it entails, which means that you are in full possession of your being. This house corresponds with Taurus.

As a quick note, of course, specific possessions are also found in the Second House, and these can run the gamut from earned income, the wealth you were born into, any debts you may have accrued, and so on. This house refers to all you own, both in the tangible and intangible sense.

- **The Third House**

This house is often referred to as the House of Communication, which means any and all communication that occurs between the self and anyone that person holds dear, such as brothers and sisters, schoolmates, or even neighbors. Communication here is meant in both the written and verbal sense, so intentionality is a big part of it. In general, it is meant to highlight the role of intelligence in one's life by underscoring the importance of any mental connections one makes with others. The Third House is ruled by Gemini together with the planet Mercury.

The House of Communication effectively underscores the importance of early education in how we can think and communicate with others, and even traveling to different environments falls within this rubric since external forces also shape this particular capacity. Basically, our ability to listen, think, process, and share falls under the Third House.

- **The Fourth House**

The Fourth House is more literal than the House of the Home. This alludes to any place where we can put down our roots. As we lay our foundation and plant ourselves firmly onto the ground, there is a circular nature to our journey. The Fourth House addresses our beginning, as well as old age, and our final resting place. This house is ruled by Cancer and the Moon.

So, this idea of the Fourth House refers to something concrete but also more conceptual since it relates more clearly to a period when and where we feel grounded. A sense of peace follows, and that is definitely the kind of energy that this particular house manifests. When you can create or find a home, it means you can find a meeting place, a sanctuary of sorts for yourself and others.

- **The Fifth House**

The Fifth House is also referred to as the House of Pleasure. Here, *pleasure* means both bodily and intellectually spurred pleasure. Whenever you have a burst of creativity and can perform the simple act of creating anything, this is a form of pleasure. So, while this house does, in fact, refer more concretely to the acts of procreation and children, it also addresses the creation of arts and culture. This is the house that spurs questions of self-satisfaction and how that could be derived in your everyday life. The Fifth House is ruled by the star sign Leo and the Sun.

So, romantic affairs definitely fall under this house, but emotional satisfaction can be derived in various ways. It can refer to acts that some people might call vices, such as gambling and the willingness to take risks. It also refers to more bucolic activities, like games and hobbies, or anything you may find engaging.

- **The Sixth House**

The last of the personal houses, the Sixth House, is also called the House of Health. Of course, it refers to your physical integrity, but it also encompasses one's ability to maintain good health in the face of adversity. Whether there is a moment of personal crisis, a health scare, or a severe reversal of fortune, these changes are all tracked by the Sixth House. Our ability to prioritize our health inevitably defines the kind of person we become, so this is an especially important house within the realm of astrology. The Sixth House is ruled by the star sign Virgo and the planet Mercury.

Interpersonal Houses

Houses seven through twelve are called the interpersonal houses, which tend to govern our relationships, travels, professional journeys, relationship with society, and spirituality over the course of our life. If a person has a lot of planets in these houses, they may be career-focused, meaning they have effectively left the past behind and focus solely on their present.

- **The Seventh House**

This is typically referred to as the House of Partnership. This is the house in which we begin to move away from the self and toward how we interact with another, namely, a partner. It also points to one's desire to accomplish something, whether it is for the sake of their relationship or society. When we can contribute to a cause or help someone else, we feel that we have a concrete purpose in life. This is the kind of work that the Seventh House tends to dominate. It is ruled by the star sign Libra and the planet Venus.

This is not to say that the Seventh House focuses solely on these lighter elements. It also encompasses the darker aspects of our relationships with others. Toxic romantic partners, divorces, and even lawsuits fall under this house.

- **The Eighth House**

This house is sometimes called the House of Sex. Here, the relationships previously alluded to are put under a microscope, and the house rules over these interactions and how they can allow us to either grow or falter. It is important to note that it does not only allude to bodily pleasure, but the Eighth House also focuses on any aspect of our life that means we are entwined with someone else. So, even things like inheritance, alimony, taxes, or any kind of financial support can fall under this house. It is ruled by Scorpio and the planets Mars and Pluto.

Unlike the House of Pleasure, creative pursuits aren't underscored here. Rather, this house focuses on how our relationships with these tangible assets, be they monetary or bodily, relate to our personal journey.

- **The Ninth House**

This is also called the House of Philosophy. As you have probably guessed, this house indicates our search for meaning and how that influences our life trajectory. By trying to understand the things we see and feel around us, we are also probing deeper into the meaning of life, even if it may not seem that way at first. This house is ruled by the star sign Sagittarius and the planet Jupiter.

While we may learn everything, for example, at school, coming face to face with our ideals and the compromises we sometimes have to make is a big part of this sign. The Ninth House also governs our quest for spirituality and, ultimately, how we understand the world will be governed by this house.

- **The Tenth House**

The Tenth House is also called the House of Social Status. It governs where we are regarding our career path and our general place in society. It also rules how we interact with our communities at large or any fame or renown that may have become part of who we are. So, achievement is deeply tied to this house which, in turn, informs us of how we see ourselves and how the community sees us. It is ruled by the star sign Capricorn and the planet Saturn.

Basically, our relationship with the individual or the group is highlighted by the Tenth House. For those interested in making an impact, paying special attention to this part of the birth chart is important. Social status here does not mean the capitalist sense of the word, but rather how we can lead fruitful lives in the service of others.

- **The Eleventh House**

This house, also referred to as the House of Friends, understands the power of the collective, and is thus informed by the idea that there is strength in numbers. It can refer to things like clubs, organizations, social groups, and even professional associations. The underlying concept of the Eleventh House is that the group can define what individuals are capable of doing. It is ruled by Aquarius and the planets Saturn and Uranus.

The Eleventh House argues that our desire to work toward the greater good with our network of friends is our humanity manifesting that particular energy. While the individual's work is important, it holds that the total sum of everyone's efforts will have the greatest impact on the world.

- **The Twelfth House**

The last of the houses is called the House of the Unconscious. This means the realm of sorrow or anything unseen by the naked eye. This state can help us succeed or make do with our failures. Basically, the two polar opposites of success and failure tend to fall within the realms of this house. When we think about our strengths or weaknesses, we are essentially thinking about The Twelfth House. It is ruled by Pisces as well as the planets Jupiter and Neptune.

Working in Tandem

The twelve houses inform and underscore different elements of our personalities and how we can develop in the future. Each one on its own is simply one piece of the puzzle, and you need to look at them collectively in a birth chart to understand the different meanings they embody.

Some people's birth charts will heavily gravitate toward other houses, which is completely normal. If one house in your birth chart currently has no planets, then that is okay. This is important information to hold onto because it shows how you currently relate to that part of your life, and you will be allowed to consider how to change it.

Each of these houses is responsible for emanating specific energy from our being that best informs who we are and how we live our lives. Some people feel that the information presented by houses is fairly concrete; therefore, our entire life is already accounted for, without any room for improvisation. Of course, this is a big mistake. Astrology is a means to understand and guide how we wish to behave or present ourselves in the future. Few things are set in stone, and life is full of surprises. Astrology allows you to explore what you would like to do next.

A birth chart is basically a zodiac wheel that follows the earth's yearly trip around the Sun, which is why it is divided into twelve ellipses, each corresponding to a particular house. Through the unique prism of these wheels, you can see different ways of looking at your personality. The zodiac sign is, ultimately, just one part of the equation. The rest of the information comes from the houses and the planets that reside within each, as sketched throughout the chart.

Therefore, the twelve houses collectively represent all aspects of human life and, when viewed in tandem, can provide you with invaluable information moving forward. The planets will reveal themselves rather emphatically in different areas of your life, as represented by the houses and where they fall on your natal chart. An important note about houses and energies is that they do not really emanate energies in that way, adding color or flow into your life. Rather, the energies tend to manifest within each of these houses. So, each house not only represents different areas of your life but your own experience of it. As you look throughout the chart, whether on your own or with the astrologer, you can figure out how the different pieces fit together and decide how you would like to move forward.

Chapter 5:
Discovering Your Sun Sign

Sun signs are vital in astrology as they represent a person's true identity. Although there are various types of zodiac signs, Sun signs are known to be the most common and popular ones. They are usually the first thing that comes to mind when someone asks you, "What is your zodiac sign?" Just like the sun shines every morning in the sky, your Sun sign is the part of you that shines out to the world. It is your essence and the driving force that allows you to express yourself and showcase your qualities and who you really are. Your Sun sign is the answer to "who are you truly?" Each person has their own unique personality traits that set them apart and showcase their individuality. Your Sun sign represents the qualities that define your truest self. It can show you your potential and who you can be. It opens up a world of possibilities and shows you the impact you can leave on the world.

In this chapter, we will discuss the 12 Sun signs so you can learn more about your sign and your various interesting qualities.

Aries (March 21 – April 19)

Nickname: The fierce fire sign

Zodiac Symbol: The Ram

Glyph: ♈

Identity: Aries are known to be competitive and must always be number one in everything. So, it is quite fitting that it is the first sun sign in the zodiac. Their boldness, ambitions, stubbornness, and occasional ruthlessness are the qualities that drive them to climb to the top and be the best. They are true individuals who are never afraid to be themselves. An Aries is known for their courage and fearlessness. They jump head first and are never afraid to take a risk. Being natural-born leaders, Aries will often take charge because they believe they can do anything they want. Ruled by Mars, the planet named after the god of war, Aries are known for their explosive temper and are always ready for battle.

Aries Role in Society

This competitive sign is only after one goal, to be the best. For this reason, you will often find Aries in leadership positions. They are energetic, dynamic, confident, and spontaneous, which makes them an inspiration to everyone around them.

Famous Aries

- Reese Witherspoon
- Elton John
- Sarah Jessica Parker
- Keira Knightley
- Mariah Carey
- Lady Gaga
- Pharrell
- Kristen Stewart
- Emma Watson
- Fergie

Professions
- Soldier
- Politician
- Entrepreneur
- Race car driver
- Personal trainer

Struggles: Aries struggle with finishing projects because they are extremely impatient and easily get bored. They crave novelty which is often why they leave projects unfinished to start new ones. Because they often juggle many things at once, Aries can forget to relax and burn themselves out.

Positive Traits
- Courageous
- Energetic
- Natural Leaders
- Confident
- Optimistic
- Passionate
- Independent
- Generous
- Honest
- Organized

Negative Traits
- Reckless
- Impulsive
- Impatient
- Angry
- Aggressive
- Selfish
- Competitive
- Attention-seeker

Taurus (April 20–May 20)

Nickname: The sensual sign

Symbol: Bull

Glyph: ♉

Identity: Taureans thrive in routine, stability, and familiar environments. Just like Aries, they are stubborn and will succeed in anything they set their mind to. However, they do not have Aries' fiery attitude. In fact, Taureans move at a slower pace. They usually enjoy relaxation and being in quiet and soothing environments. Ruled by Venus, Taureans are known to be the most sensual sign in the zodiac. They love luxury, comfort, and beauty.

Taurus Role in Society

Taureans are dependable individuals because of how stable they are. People often rely on them; they are always the "rock" others can lean on in times of need. People always depend on the Taureans in the group when it comes to group projects, whether at work or school. Thanks to their determination and productivity, they can serve as a strong foundation in any group project.

Famous Taureans

- Queen Elizabeth II
- Robert Pattinson
- The Rock
- Channing Tatum
- Adele
- George Clooney
- Jon Cena
- Barbra Streisand
- Janet Jackson
- Sam Smith

Professions

- Lawyer
- Chef

- Designer
- Teacher
- Engineer

Struggles: Taureans struggle with a few things. Jealousy is one of their biggest struggles, whether in romantic relationships or when someone has something they want. They can also be very stubborn, which sometimes costs them. Additionally, Taureans move slowly and may require encouragement and motivation to keep going.

Positive Traits
- Sensual
- Reliable
- Patient
- Kind
- Intelligent
- Organized
- Hard-working
- Honest

Negative Traits
- Stubborn
- Lazy
- Jealous
- Perfectionist
- Possessive

Gemini (May 21–June 21)

Nickname: The curious

Symbol: Twins

Glyph: ♊

Identity: Geminis are known for their communication skills. They are social butterflies who love meeting new people. Geminis' whole identity revolves around their chatty and charming attitude. They are quick-witted and can talk about different topics and strike up conversations with anyone they meet. This is probably the result of their curious, knowledgeable, and intellectual nature.

Gemini's Role in Society

Geminis love to throw parties and do anything that can bring everyone together. They make friends with every stranger they meet. Well-spoken, social, and outgoing, they are the life of the party, and they bring excitement and fun conversations wherever they go.

Famous Geminis

- Johnny Depp
- Marilyn Monroe
- John F. Kennedy
- Angelina Jolie
- Prince
- Morgan Freeman
- Tom Holland
- Helena Bonham Carter
- Paul McCartney
- Chris Evans

Professions

- Teacher
- Social worker
- Architect

- Technical support
- Stockbroker

Struggles: Geminis struggle to keep things to themselves. They love gossiping and chatting but do not understand that other people's secrets are not theirs to share. They do not know where to draw the line between what to share and what to keep to themselves.

Positive Traits
- Curious
- Sociable
- Creative
- Sense of humor
- Intellectual
- Charismatic
- Savvy

Negative Traits
- Gossip
- Immature
- Mood swings
- Impulsive
- Superficial

Cancer (June 22–July 22)

Nickname: The heartfelt

Symbol: Crab

Glyph: ♋

Identity: If you see a sensitive person, they are most likely Cancer. Cancers are always aware of their environment and can pick up on other people's emotions. They are so intuitive that you may mistake them for psychics. Home means a lot to Cancer; it is their haven where they can rest and self-reflect. They create strong bonds thanks to their loyalty and emotional depth.

Cancer's Role in Society

Cancers are always there for the people they care about. You can depend on them for anything. They aim to spread love to everyone they meet. They love the idea of a family and often play the role of the caregiver.

Famous Cancers

- Meryl Streep
- Margot Robbie
- Chris Pratt
- Selena Gomez
- Ariana Grande
- Lana Del Ray
- Tom Hanks
- Tom Cruise
- Will Ferrell
- Gisele Bündchen

Professions

- Teacher
- Lawyer
- Gardner
- Social worker

- Childcare
- Human resources

Struggles: Due to their extra sensitive nature, Cancers are easily offended. They struggle to handle criticism or good-natured teasing.

Positive Traits
- Caring
- Loyal
- Protective
- Faithful
- Charming
- Sentimental
- Intuitive

Negative Traits
- Mood swings
- Insecure
- Vengeful
- Overly-sensitive
- Manipulative
- Pessimistic\

Leo (July 23–August 22)

Nickname: Spot-light loving

Symbol: Lion

Glyph: ♌

Identity: The celebrities of the zodiac signs, Leos, love to be the center of attention and under the spotlight. Just like their animal symbol, Leos are dominant and natural-born leaders. In their heads, Leos are celebrities and believe they should be treated like superstars. They are extremely confident and proud, but their pride and ego can get the best of them on occasion.

Leo's Role in Society

These superstars have a mesmerizing charisma that people often gravitate towards. Similar to the lion, Leos are extremely courageous, and they inspire everyone around them with their courage. They are true individuals who stand out and make an impact in society through their creative power.

Famous Leos

- Jennifer Lopez
- Daniel Radcliffe
- Mick Jagger
- Helen Mirren
- Sandra Bullock
- Terry Crews
- Jason Momoa
- Barack Obama
- Charlize Theron
- Chris Hemsworth

Professions

- Real estate agent
- Performer
- Fashion designer

- CEO
- Salesperson
- Tour guide

Struggles: Leos tend to spend all their time in the spotlight. They forget to take some time off to relax and eventually burn themselves out.

Positive Traits
- Natural-born leaders
- Strong
- Generous
- Protective
- Passionate
- Determined
- Ambitious
- Creative
- Honest
- Friendly

Negative Traits
- Arrogant
- Attention-seekers
- Stubborn
- Lazy
- Inflexible
- Competitive
- Jealous
- Proud

Virgo (August 23–September 22)

Nickname: Detail-oriented

Symbol: The virgin

Glyph: ♍

Identity: Virgos are known for being practical, logical, and dedicated. They are also detail-oriented and never leave anything to chance. Grounded and realistic, this practical sign never loses its head in the clouds. Honest and straightforward, Virgos stick to the truth even if it hurts. They are kind and supportive and use their problem-solving abilities to help their friends.

Virgo's Role in Society

Virgo's goal is to spread peace to everyone around them. They work hard on any skill they learn until they achieve perfection. As a result, at work, they usually play a vital role and ensure everything runs smoothly.

Famous Virgos

- Beyonce
- Blake Lively
- John Mulaney
- Cameron Diaz
- Zendaya
- Keanu Reeves
- Salma Hayek
- Idris Elba
- Colin Firth
- Pink

Professions

- Journalist
- Writer
- Critic
- Editor

- Detective
- Technician
- Teacher
- Translator

Struggles: Perfection does not exist, but Virgos refuse to see this fact. Their need to pay attention to every detail can be exhausting. They are afraid to make mistakes and can take themselves too seriously and forget to have fun.

Positive Traits
- Hard-working
- Kind
- Patient
- Creative
- Reliable
- Helpful
- Responsible
- Modest
- Intelligent
- Calm

Negative Traits
- Stubborn
- Picky
- People-pleasers
- Perfectionist
- Judgmental
- Anxious

Libra (September 23–October 23)

Nickname: The social butterfly

Symbol: The scales

Glyph: ♎

Identity: Just like their symbol, the scale, Libras are fair and always want to achieve justice. They try to find balance in various areas of their life. Libras are often accused of being indecisive because they take time to decide. However, they simply like to do that to weigh all their options. Ruled by Venus, Libra loves romance, harmony, luxury, and beauty. Libras are also known to be very social and love to surround themselves with people who like to have fun and avoid conflict.

Libra's Role in Society

Libras are fair idealists and are interested in achieving justice. They work toward fighting injustice because they believe they can make the world a better place. Libras are considered great teammates and will stand up to those in power when they feel someone is treated unfairly.

Famous Libras

- Serena Williams
- Will Smith
- Gwyneth Paltrow
- Hilary Duff
- Halsey
- Eminem
- Hugh Jackman
- John Krasinski
- Zac Efron
- Tyler Posey

Professions

- Dancer
- Negotiator

- Salesperson
- Host
- Diplomat
- Travel agent
- Supervisor

Struggles: Libras struggle to make decisions, whether big or small, because they have to consider all the pros and cons. This can be very exhausting as they are always afraid of making a decision they will regret. They need to understand that it is okay to make the wrong decisions every now and then. How else will they learn?

Positive Traits
- Fair
- Perfectionist
- Intelligent
- Social
- Charming
- Great listener
- Sense of humor
- Romantic
- Intuitive

Negative Traits
- Vain
- Indecisive
- Lazy
- Self-pity
- Superficial

Scorpio (October 24–November 21)

Nickname: The magnetic

Symbol: Scorpion

Glyph: ♏

Identity: Scorpios are the most determined and focused of all the signs. They will work hard, plot, and research to find something or get what they want. Extremely calculating, Scorpios treat life like a chess game and often try to be a few steps ahead of their opponent. Mysterious and enigmatic, Scorpios can be very secretive, which makes them attractive and appealing to others.

Scorpio's Role in Society

Whenever a Scorpio is passionate about a cause, they will fight for it. They do not care about the consequences. Fearless and unstoppable, they are relentless warriors who will never give up until their side wins. They believe that they can make a difference in the world through passion.

Famous Scorpios

- Leonardo DiCaprio
- Ryan Reynolds
- Katy Perry
- Drake
- Julia Roberts
- Winona Ryder
- Penn Badgley
- Emma Stone
- Ryan Gosling
- Anne Hathaway

Professions

- Surgeon
- Lawyer
- Scientist

- Detective
- Educator

Struggles: Scorpios are extremely focused, which can lead them to become a little obsessive. They never take a step back and look at the big picture.

Positive Traits

- Loyal
- Ambitious
- Determined
- Honest
- Curious
- Passionate
- Courageous
- Independent
- Persistent

Negative Traits

- Jealous
- Stubborn
- Possessive
- Controlling
- Intimidating
- Resentful

Sagittarius (November 22–December 21)

Nickname: The adventurous

Symbol: The archer

Glyph: ♐

Identity: Sagittarius is the most unique zodiac sign because of its blend of characteristics. Some of Sagittarius's unique qualities that make them stand out are adaptability, curiosity, passion, and intensity. Their adventurous spirit often leads them to explore places no one else would dare approach. This can be the result of their curious and energetic nature which loves traveling and venturing to new places.

Sagittarius Role in Society

Optimistic with childlike curiosity, they want to make people curious like them. They are always looking to inspire others and ignite their spirits. Witty and reliable, they bring peace whenever there is conflict or tension.

Famous Sagittarius

- Scarlett Johansson
- Miley Cyrus
- Don Cheadle
- Ben Stiller
- Lucy Liu
- Britney Spears
- Amanda Seyfried
- Taylor Swift
- Jamie Foxx
- Brad Pitt

Professions

- Editor
- Public relations
- Animal trainer

- Minister

Struggles: Sagittarius is adventurous and always on the lookout for something more interesting to do. However, this can make them flaky and constantly struggle to meet their plans.

Positive Traits
- Curious
- Active
- Adventurous
- Ambitious
- Friendly
- Deep thinkers
- Adaptable
- Visionary
- Bold

Negative Traits
- Restless
- Rude
- Short-tempered
- Arrogant
- Inconsistent
- Reckless
- Stubborn
- Blunt

Capricorns (December 22–January 19)

Nickname: The motivated

Symbol: The goat

Glyph: ♑

Identity: If you have ever spent time with a Capricorn, you have probably noticed that there is something special about them. It can be their fearlessness, ambition, resilience, wild side, or the fact that they never give up despite their adversity. At first glance, Capricorns may seem reserved and conservative. But they have a rebellious spirit and love to let loose every time. Traditional, responsible, and independent, Capricorns are great leaders. They are often realistic with their plans and learn from their mistakes.

Capricorn's Role in Society

Capricorns are extremely nurturing and supportive to their loved ones. The people in their lives know they can depend on them for anything. They work hard, often occupy positions of authority, and are highly respected by others.

Famous Capricorns

- Kate Middleton
- Finn Wolfhard
- Kit Harington
- Jared Leto
- Diane Keaton
- Zayn Malik
- Regina King
- Kate Moss
- Jim Carrey
- Betty White

Professions

- IT
- Editor
- Manager

- Banker
- Administrator

Struggles: Capricorns work hard but forget that playing hard is essential too. They tend to neglect themselves and other aspects of their lives because they can be workaholics. They should pay more attention to themselves and their relationships.

Positive Traits
- Realist
- Ambitious
- Persistent
- Loyal
- Discipline
- Responsible
- Team player
- Reliable
- Intelligent

Negative Traits
- Stubborn
- Pessimistic
- Serious
- Sensitive
- Picky
- Unforgiving

Aquarius (January 20–February 18)

Nickname: The quirky

Symbol: Water-bearer

Glyph: ♒

Identity: Eccentric and quirky, Aquarians definitely stand out. They are the rebels who fight for freedom. However, they can often be quiet and shy as well. Intellectual, idealistic, and deep thinkers who will never stop fighting for what they believe in. They are spontaneous, live life to the fullest, and are determined to never waste their time. Free-spirited, Aquarians believe they can change the world. They do not live by anyone's rules but their own.

Aquarius Role in Society

Aquarians love being a part of a community where they can make an impact and positive changes. They are compassionate and care about humanitarian causes. They are often the ones volunteering for social causes, and they believe they can make a difference in the world.

Famous Aquarians

- Harry Styles
- Oprah Winfrey
- Shakira
- Alicia Keys
- Michael B. Jordan
- Jennifer Aniston
- The Weekend
- Chris Rock
- Elizabeth Olsen
- Tom Hiddleston

Professions

- Inventor
- Musician
- Aviator

- Scientist
- Designer

Struggles: Unlike Leos, who thrive under attention, Aquarians struggle with being in the spotlight. They also usually guard themselves and struggle with warming up to people.

Positive Traits
- Creative
- Open-minded
- Intelligent
- Free-spirited
- Ambitious
- Original
- Friendly
- Easygoing

Negative Traits
- Inconsistent
- Unpredictable
- Impulsive
- Stubborn
- Idealistic
- Detached
- Insensitive
- Unpredictable

Pisces (February 19–March 20)

Nickname: The dreamy

Symbol: Fish

Glyph: ♓

Identity: Pisces is dreamy, and their heads are often between reality and fantasy. Compassionate, sensitive, and extremely empathetic, they can be overwhelmed by emotions. They often live in a world they have built in their imagination and are ruled by dreams and creativity. They are so optimistic that some people see them as delusional. Pisces are selfless and helpful and surround themselves with people from all walks of life.

Pisces' Role in Society

Pisces can inspire and connect with people through art, poetry, or any form of artistic creativity. Well-intentioned and compassionate, Pisces will do anything for others, even if it inconveniences them.

Famous Pisces

- Justin Bieber
- Rihanna
- Emily Blunt
- Drew Barrymore
- Millie Bobby Brown
- Eva Langoria
- Camila Cabello
- Adam Levine
- Carrie Underwood
- Bad Bunny

Professions

- Psychologist
- Nurse
- Vet

- Artist
- Philanthropist
- Physical therapist

Struggles: Pisces are generous and sweet-natured but can also be gullible. They struggle with setting boundaries and saying "no," which leads others to take advantage of them.

Positive Traits
- Generous
- Sensitive
- Empathetic
- Creative
- Compassionate
- Intuitive
- Devoted
- Forgiving
- Romantic
- Strong
- Natural leaders

Negative Traits
- Gullible
- Closed off
- Too emotional
- Moody
- Lazy
- Idealistic

Your Sun sign can teach you so much about your personality and potential. It can serve as a guide to help you work on your weaknesses and find a career where you can thrive. Learning about these signs can also help you to better understand the people in your life and what you can do for them when they are struggling. Embrace who you are and work on what you can be.

Chapter 6:
Identifying Your Moon Sign

Similar to the Moon, a part of us is always hidden. This part is kept from the rest of the world and only surfaces when you are alone. To better understand who you are and unveil your deepest self, the part of you that no one can see, you need to discover your Moon sign. Most people are familiar with the Sun sign as it is the one that reflects their personality traits and who they are to the world. Although Moon signs are not as popular as Sun signs, they impact one's character and influence our lives more than them. There are two sides to each person's personality. One is governed by the Sun, while the Moon governs the other.

The Moon's presence in the zodiac at your moment of birth is what determines your Moon sign. It represents the soul's identity, a part of you located deep down that sometimes you may not even be aware of, but it greatly impacts your emotions.

While the Sun sign is responsible for your identity and basic self, the Moon sign is responsible for your emotional responses and inner and hidden self. It reflects who you are when no one is around, while the Sun sign is who you are around other people. Only those closest to you can see your Moon sign personality. Your Moon sign reflects who you are truly in your comfort zone, while your Sun sign reflects your path, mission, and true purpose in life. Your Sun sign represents your will, ego, and fundamental personality. It mainly represents who you think you are. Your Moon sign is your subconscious self and how you react to the world around you.

To learn about your Moon sign, check your birth chart or go online and enter your birth details to find out the Moon's exact location at the time of your birth. In this chapter, we will discuss the Moon's signs so you can learn about the soul of your true identity.

Aries Moon

Nickname: Desire

Zodiac Symbol: The Ram

Glyph: ♈

Identity: Similar to its Sun sign, Moon Aries is also known to be fiery and impulsive. They usually go after what their heart desires and lead exciting and spontaneous lives. Aries Moon usually represents your impatient inner child who must always get everything they want. It is all about instant gratification for this sign. Aries Moon is usually a quick thinker but does not concern themselves with small details. Trouble seems to follow them wherever they go, or maybe they are the ones who invite it? With Aries Moon, what you see is always what you get.

Aries Moon's Role in Society

Aries Moon individuals are very giving when it comes to their loved ones. They enjoy being themselves at all times and will resent anyone who tries to restrict them or interfere with their freedom. Although it is very easy to hurt Aries Moon's feelings, they can forgive you if they see you remorseful.

Famous Aries Moon

- Angelina Jolie
- Tom Hiddleston
- Rihanna
- Salma Hayek
- Pink
- Joaquin Phoenix
- Eva Langoria

- Jared Leto
- Daniel Craig
- Chris Rock

Professions
- Manager
- Executive
- Business owner
- Mechanic
- Engineer

Struggles: Aries Moon people do not accept failure, and their desire to succeed can lead them to lose their temper or be hysterical.

Positive Traits
- Optimistic
- Self-sufficient
- Enthusiastic
- Sociable
- Energetic
- Lively
- Outspoken
- Sincere

Negative Traits
- Restless
- Inconsistent
- Emotionally exhausting
- Mean
- Impatient

Taurus Moon

Nickname: Determination

Symbol: Bull

Glyph: ♉

Identity: Taurus Moon individuals are very calm and rarely get angry. They usually enjoy a luxurious lifestyle and cozy environments. These individuals are down to Earth and thrive in routine and stability. They are also extremely stubborn, and once they set their mind on something, they never waver.

Taurus Moon's Role in Society

People born under this sign are loyal and devoted to their loved ones. They thrive on developing emotional connections and nurturing relationships with others. Emotionally strong, kind, and loyal, they form bonds that can last a lifetime.

Famous Taurus Moon

- Robert Downey Jr
- Adam Driver
- Colin Firth
- Meryl Streep
- Demi Moore
- Zendaya
- Jamie Foxx
- Cameron Diaz
- Brendan Fraser
- David Boreanaz

Professions

- Artist
- Designer
- Jeweler
- Real estate agent
- Business

Struggles: Taurus Moon individuals struggle to express their emotions. They do not know how to openly talk about their problems, even to their loved ones.

Positive Traits
- Stable
- Balanced
- Focused
- Patient
- Strong
- Confident
- Loyal
- Gentle
- Reliable

Negative Traits
- Shy
- Stubborn
- Materialistic
- Lazy

Gemini Moon

Nickname: Communication

Symbol: Twins

Glyph: ♊

Identity: Free-spirited; these individuals often express themselves in a non-restricted and light manner. They thrive on intellectual and witty conversations. When communicating, they usually use information and facts. They love the spotlight and often enjoy having people fight for their attention. They can be shallow, so they usually choose partners based on what they find interesting rather than people with whom they can form deep connections.

Lunar Gemini's Role in Society

People often feel at ease around Gemini Moon individuals because of their ability to relate to others' opinions and experiences. They enjoy a good debate and may sometimes try to influence other people's opinions. Since Gemini's symbol is twins, Gemini Moon individuals are always looking for their "twin" or their other half.

Famous Lunar Geminis

- Barack Obama
- Rachel McAdams
- Jeremy Renner
- Olivia Wilde
- Hugh Jackman
- Jake Gyllenhaal
- Kylie Minogue
- Jennifer Garner
- Jonathan Groff
- Brooke Shields

Professions

- Dancer
- Librarian
- Investor

- Accountant
- Research worker
- Journalist

Struggles: Instead of confronting their feelings, people born under this sign usually dance around the subject. They struggle to understand their true feelings.

Positive Traits
- Happy
- Confident
- Realistic
- Practical
- Sociable

Negative Traits
- Deceptive
- Shallow
- Moody
- Mysterious

Cancer Moon

Nickname: Solicitude

Symbol: Crab

Glyph: ♋

Identity: People born under this sign are extremely empathetic. They can sense the energy in the room and are sensitive to other people's feelings. Trust is essential for them, and they often gravitate toward relationships where they feel supported and safe. Cancer Moon individuals are giving, nurturing, and maternal. The Moon rules the Sun sign Cancer, so if you were born under a Cancer or Cancer Moon, you would be affected by the different moon phases.

Cancer Moon's Role in Society

Cancer Moon individuals are extremely dependable and create deep relationships. They are often there for the people in their life to help them solve their problems and to provide helpful advice.

Famous Lunar Cancers

- Taylor Swift
- Dua Lipa
- Keanu Reeves
- Shakira
- Jack White
- Michael B Jordan
- Melissa McCarthy
- Kerry Washington
- Colin Farrell
- Elizabeth Olsen

Professions

- Poets
- Artists
- Musicians
- Photographer

- Psychologist
- Nurses

Struggles: They often struggle to move on and can dwell for a long time over past pain. Opening up does not come easily to Cancer Moon because they do not like to appear vulnerable.

Positive Traits
- Compassionate
- Kind
- Sympathetic
- Peaceful
- Great memory
- Romantic
- Gentle
- Affectionate
- Giving
- Tenacious
- Intuitive
- Sense of humor

Negative Traits
- Manipulative
- Victim mentality
- Irrational
- Moody

Leo Moon

Nickname: Freedom

Symbol: Lion

Glyph: ♌

Identity: Caring and giving, Leo Moon individuals enjoy expressing their love through lavish gifts. Like their Sun counterpart, they enjoy being the center of attention and usually have huge egos. They do not tolerate it when someone insults their ego and may even walk away for good. However, they do not make a strong impression as easily as Leo Sun, and they have to work harder to make an impact on others.

Leo Moon's Role in Society

Leo Moon individuals are considered great entertainers, and others enjoy their company. They also can make people completely rely on them.

Famous Leo Moon

- Paul McCartney
- Julia Roberts
- Tom Cruise
- Jamie Dornan
- Megan Fox
- Chris Martin
- Maisie Williams
- Liam Hemsworth
- Hugh Laurie
- Cobie Smulders

Professions

- Comedians
- Schools principles
- Athletes
- Boxers

- Midwives
- Astrologers
- Theater workers

Struggles: They may struggle with having huge egos that make them only focus on themselves and ignore everyone else around them.

Positive Traits
- Warm
- Creative
- Assertive
- Strong
- Decisive
- Generous
- Optimistic
- Stylish
- Determined
- Fair
- Proud

Negative Traits
- Controlling
- Bossy
- Lazy
- Dramatic

Virgo Moon

Nickname: Criticism

Symbol: The virgin

Glyph: ♍

Identity: Virgo Moon individuals thrive in an organized and structured environment. They enjoy everyday activities others find tedious, like paying the bills or running errands. Many Virgo Moon individuals are pretty content to lead a simple life and stay away from any attention.

Virgo Moon's Role in Society

They can create dynamic and comprehensive systems to help others. In fact, Virgo Moon people are always there to lend a hand, and they only feel fulfilled when they are helpful.

Famous Lunar Virgo

- Dolly Parton
- Michael Fassbender
- Madonna
- Chris Hemsworth
- Betty White
- Serena Williams
- Rami Malek
- John Travolta
- Zac Efron
- Jim Sturgess

Professions

- Banker
- Bookkeeper
- Inventor
- Literary critic
- Liberian
- Real estate agent

Struggles: Virgo Moon people can be overwhelmed with stress and worry and may struggle to handle pressure.

Positive Traits
- Fair-minded
- Compassionate
- Patient
- Logical
- Organized
- Helpful
- Social

Negative Traits
- Picky
- Critical
- Extra sensitive
- Prejudiced
- Over-thinker
- Low self-esteem

Libra Moon

Nickname: Charm

Symbol: The scales

Glyph: ♎

Identity: Libra Moon people only feel secure and complete when they have someone to share their lives with. They are usually classy and gentle, which is why many people are often attracted to them. Social interactions with loved ones are vital for Libra Moon as this is where they find emotional fulfillment. They are not the most committed individuals in relationships and usually jump from one relationship to the other.

Libra Moon's Role in Society

They are great debaters and have a knack for justice, so they will often defend their loved ones and will not give up until they win. Just as they love to have the best of everything, they enjoy spoiling the people in their lives with luxurious gifts and meals.

Famous Lunar Librax

- Leonardo DiCaprio
- Kate Winslet
- Sylvia Plath
- Walt Disney
- Nicolas Cage
- Alec Baldwin
- Bruce Springsteen
- Gena Davis
- Louis Armstrong
- Sylvester Stallone

Professions

- Banker
- Any job in finance

Struggles: Libra Moon people are idealists and are constantly chasing perfection. This can be exhausting and can prevent them from enjoying their lives.

Positive Traits
- Sympathetic
- Witty
- Social
- Charming
- Attractive
- Rational
- Diplomatic
- Creative

Negative Traits
- Critical
- Emotionless
- Passive-aggressive
- Anxious
- Dependent
- Self-indulgent
- People pleasers

Scorpio Moon

Nickname: Ulterior motivation

Symbol: Scorpion

Glyph: ♏

Identity: Scorpio Moon individuals are only comfortable when their emotions are intense. In fact, they are always seeking intense experiences and emotional excitement. They are not ones to be fooled by someone's appearance, and they can read people and understand them on a deeper level. They thrive in meaningful relationships and often have an all-or-nothing attitude.

Lunar Scorpio Role in Society

People are either attracted to or intimidated by a Scorpio Moon because of their ability to see through people's facades. Thanks to their strong intuition, many people often rely on them and trust their insight.

Famous Lunar Scorpio

- Lady Gaga
- Beyonce
- Katy Perry
- James Dean
- Jason Momoa
- Bob Marley
- Mila Kunis
- Miley Cyrus
- Selma Blair
- Elizabeth Taylor

Professions

- Surgeon
- Teacher
- Counselor
- Soldier

- Psychologist
- Engineer

Struggles: They struggle to trust others and only let people they fully trust into their lives. Scorpio Moon's secretive nature can sometimes prevent them from connecting with their loved ones.

Positive Traits
- Intuitive
- Strong
- Intelligent
- Deep
- Powerful

Negative Traits
- Secretive
- Deceitful
- Resentful
- Moody
- Vengeful
- Needy

Sagittarius Moon

Nickname: Enthusiasm

Symbol: A mythical centaur or Archer

Glyph: ♐

Identity: Sagittarius Moon is at their best when they feel free. If anything or anyone jeopardizes their sense of freedom, they can become very unhappy. They enjoy leading an active life, so you will often find them traveling to see the world or going out to meet new people. With their infectious optimism, these individuals believe in happy endings and that everything eventually works out. Straightforward and often blunt, they express themselves directly without playing mind games or dancing around the subject.

Sagittarius Moon's Role in Society

Sagittarius Moon people are very helpful and often act as teachers to their loved ones by guiding or helping them learn new things. Fair and just, they will help and fight for anyone experiencing injustice.

Famous Sagittarius Moon

- Oprah Winfrey
- Jennifer Aniston
- Nicole Kidman
- John Mulaney
- Kevin Costner
- Ellie Goulding
- Zoe Saldana
- Anthony Hopkins
- Adele
- Neil Patrick Harris

Professions

- Teacher
- Counselor
- Social worker

- Journalist
- Entertainer
- Travel agent
- Tour guide

Struggles: Sometimes, they dominate the conversation and can be condescending to those around them. They usually act as if they are the smartest people in the room. In most cases, they get away with this attitude because of their fun and cheerful personality.

Positive Traits
- Easy going
- Cheerful
- Intelligent
- Optimistic
- Upbeat
- Free-spirited
- Adaptable
- Daring
- Independent

Negative Traits
- Irresponsible
- Forgetful
- Impulsive
- Blunt
- Explosive temper
- Impatient

Capricorn Moon

Nickname: Management

Symbol: The goat

Glyph: ♑

Identity: Capricorn Moon is often in control of their emotions. Even when they are going through something or experiencing various feelings, they will often display a cool and collected demeanor. Realistic individuals, Capricorn Moon people often set attainable goals. They would rather play it safe than take risks. Security is essential to them, which is why they always plan ahead for their future, like saving money for retirement. Their self-worth usually depends on the respect they get from others which is why they work so hard to become successful.

Capricorn Moon's Role in Society

They are extremely responsible individuals, and they are the ones that you can usually count on in group projects. Lunar Capricorns are hard-working and dedicated, so they always manage to advance in their careers.

Famous Capricorn Moon

- Brad Pitt
- Reese Witherspoon
- Dwayne Johnson
- Johnny Depp
- Kate Hudson
- Matt Damon
- Rosamund Pike
- Gerard Butler
- Bryan Cranston
- Maya Hawke

Professions

- CEO
- Administrator

- Banker
- Designer
- Accountant
- Real estate agent

Struggles: Capricorn Moon individuals want nothing more than to achieve their goals and become successful. As a result, they may forget to relax and have fun now and then. They also build a wall around themselves and struggle to open up to others or express their emotions.

Positive Traits
- Competent
- Cool
- Collected
- Calm
- Organized
- Serious
- Ambitious

Negative Traits
- Mood swings
- Cold
- Selfish
- Calculating
- Controlling

Aquarius Moon

Nickname: Disinterest

Symbol: Water-bearer

Glyph: ♒

Identity: Aquarius Moon individuals are extremely analytical and usually observe and analyze other people's behavior. As children, these individuals always felt they were different from everyone else. On the outside, they may seem like social individuals, but, in reality, they are quite the loners. This is mainly because they never felt like they fit in with anyone. For this reason, they will do anything to stand out from the crowd and showcase their unique individuality. Aquarius Moon people believe they are better than others and often deny experiencing any negative emotions like jealousy or fear because they are above these "petty" feelings.

Aquarius Moon's Role in Society

You will often find Aquarius Moon volunteering for humanitarian causes. However, this is done for more philosophical reasons than to help others. They are extremely independent and detached and expect others to be the same. Since they often feel like they do not fit in, Aquarius Moon individuals always make sure to help others feel included. They wholeheartedly believe in equality and will fight tooth and nail for it.

Famous Aquarius Moon

- Billie Eilish
- John Lennon
- Britney Spears
- Marilyn Monroe
- Shawn Mendes
- Henry Cavill
- Princess Diana
- Gigi Hadid
- Morgan Freeman
- Tobey Maguire

Professions
- Astrologist
- Politician
- Humanitarian
- Explorer
- Teacher

Struggles: They usually struggle with being detached and distant from other people because of their huge egos and belief that they are better and above normal human emotions.

Positive Traits
- Observant
- Independent
- Loyal
- Trustworthy
- Charming
- Quirky
- Honest

Negative Traits
- Huge ego
- Proud
- Aloof
- Stubborn
- Distant
- Unreliable

Pisces Moon

Nickname: Anxiety

Symbol: Fish

Glyph: ♓

Identity: Pisces Moon individuals are probably the least practical people you will ever meet. However, they are extremely intuitive and easily see things from other people's perspectives. Although they are very funny, their sense of humor may seem odd to others. Daydreamers, these individuals require time to be alone with their imagination every day. During this time, they may come up with ideas to solve various problems, even though many of their solutions may seem unconventional. They are extremely empathetic and able to feel other people's emotions and experiences. Although they may seem gullible, many Pisces Moon individuals can sense when someone is manipulating them.

Pisces Moon's Role in Society

Pisces Moon individuals care so much about their close relationships and often make them a priority. Thanks to their empathetic nature, these individuals often want to help others and make the world a better place.

Famous Lunar Pisceans

- Edgar Allan Poe
- Leonardo Da Vinci
- Sarah Michelle Gellar
- Frank Sinatra
- Robert De Niro
- Elvis Presley
- Kathy Bates
- Audrey Hepburn
- Paul Newman
- Prince

Professions
- Actors/Actresses
- Artists
- Writers
- Musicians
- Poets
- Detectives
- Promoters

Struggles: They live in their heads more than in the real world. Often, they struggle to ground themselves and develop an escapist attitude.

Positive Traits
- Intuitive
- Compassionate
- Kind-hearted
- Sweet
- Sentimental
- Creative
- Empathic
- Loyal
- Sensitive

Negative Traits
- Secretive
- Indecisive
- Negative
- Submissive
- Sensitive

Your connection to the Moon is vital to help you better understand yourself more deeply. Naturally, you will find many similarities between your Sun and Moon signs. Although the Moon's presence impacts each sign, you will still find the Sun's sign's influence in each Lunar sign. Sun and Moon signs can help take you on a self-discovery journey to learn about your truest self and discover things you may not even be aware of.

Chapter 7: Sun-Moon Combinations I - Earth-Sun Signs

As you have likely already realized, both your Sun and Moon signs play an enormous role in determining your personality traits. Given the popularity of Sun signs, there is a good chance you already know how they affect your personality, but things can take a turn when you also consider your Moon sign.

Suppose you are an earth Sun sign, Taurus, Virgo, or Capricorn, looking to understand how your personality can change when you take your Moon sign into account. In that case, this is the chapter for you. We will look at the different Sun-Moon combinations, including each sign's good and bad traits, and figure out the perfect partner for each one. We will also offer advice to help you interact with people with these signs.

Taurus Sun-Taurus Moon: The Down-to-Earth Hand-worker

People with sun and moon in Taurus are usually hard workers.
https://unsplash.com/photos/k_T9Zj3SE8k?utm_source=unsplash&utm_medium=referral&utm_content=creditShareLink

People with both their Sun and Moon in Taurus are down-to-earth, dedicated, and hardworking. They have extraordinary focus and maintain a grounded outlook on life. They are relatively conventional and aren't fans of change. However, at the same time, they are also not easily ruffled by stressors and are solid, steadfast friends.

Good Traits: Hardworking, Persistent, Diplomatic

Taurus Sun-Taurus Moon individuals are dedicated to each activity they attempt. They are extremely eloquent, and people attentively listen when they talk. They are also calm and easygoing and can put other people at ease. They are trustworthy and reliable in their relationships and are loyal and honest with their loved ones.

Bad Traits: Materialistic, Conventional, Intolerant

People with this Sun and Moon combination often find themselves overly focused on money which may not be the best option when dealing with high-risk financial situations. They want the safety of money too badly, which can lead to them becoming materialistic. Additionally, they are highly conventional – and may find it challenging to adapt to change. They can also be intolerant towards other people, especially those with other perspectives.

Perfect Partner: Taurus Sun-Taurus Moon people are loyal and dedicated partners with a deep desire for physical and emotional intimacy. However, they can also become comfortable in routines, which can bore air and fire signs. On the other hand, water and earth signs work well with them. Their perfect partner should be able to bring a spiritual side to the relationship. High-conflict individuals are a bad match.

Advice for Taurus Sun-Taurus Moon People:

- Try to open up more to your partner. You can come across as closed off and withdrawn, especially when you keep negative feelings bottled up.
- Talk about your feelings more. Allowing frustrations to pile up can lead to emotional outbursts.
- Keep other perspectives in mind. It can be difficult to see why other people cannot find solutions to problems as easily as you, but trying to understand them will serve you well.

Advice for Dealing with Taurus Sun-Taurus Moon People:

- They are slow to adjust to change, so you should be prepared to give them the time they need.
- They appreciate consistency, steadiness, and loyalty in their personal relationships, both romantic and otherwise.
- While they are hard workers, this will not be at the cost of their personal relationships. They generally have a great work-life balance and will be able to give time to their loved ones.

Taurus Sun-Virgo Moon: The Charming Pragmatist

People with this Sun-Moon combination have a good deal of common sense and a scrutinizing mind. They are astute judges of character and err on the side of caution in whatever they do. They are naturally appealing, making it easy to charm the people around them.

Good Traits: Studious, Responsible, Observant

When given responsibilities, they can be relied on to accomplish their tasks. They have quick minds and love to read and retain material that others may find insignificant. They are very observant and analyze each decision thoroughly before committing to it.

Perfect Partner: Taurus Sun-Virgo Moon people are often attracted to people with a more happy-go-lucky personality. They are considerate, supportive, and loyal partners but look for people with similar goals and desires. They want long-term relationships and stability and are drawn to people they can shape.

Advice for Taurus Sun-Virgo Moon People:

- Do not get distracted by perfection; it can stop you from taking any kind of action.
- Remember to manage your stress. You can take your stress out on your partner without realizing it, so you should develop management strategies to prevent this from happening.
- Plan your tasks ahead of time; a routine will help you focus.

Advice for Dealing with Taurus Sun-Virgo Moon People:

- Provide them with challenges. A lack of challenges can lead to them procrastinating and falling behind on tasks.
- Be prepared for criticism. Taurus Sun-Virgo Moon individuals are perfectionists who criticize others and themselves. This can benefit their own growth but can be disturbing to others.

- They may occasionally isolate themselves from others due to their perfectionist tendencies and worries about their own skills. You will have to push them to interact with the people around them.

Taurus Sun-Capricorn Moon: The Role Model

People with this Sun-Moon combination are stable and decisive and do not waste time daydreaming. They are dependable, practical, and responsible. They are also ambitious and determined, which will help them succeed in life. They often seek to be positive role models and are honest and reliable.

Good Traits: Cautious, Humble, Reliable

Taurus Sun-Capricorn Moon people appreciate the efforts of the people around them. They are cautious, only act after thinking things through, and often have a backup plan to fall back on if things go wrong. They are very supportive and are great friends.

Bad Traits: Materialistic, Narrow-Minded, Workaholic

While they are not the most materialistic of all Taurus Sun-Moon combinations, they are still focused on achieving monetary success and afraid of poverty. This can lead to them becoming workaholics and ignoring personal relationships. They are also conservative to the point of being narrow-minded and need to feel in control of every situation.

Perfect Partner: These individuals need partners who understand their stubbornness. They are looking for a committed partner who is a doer instead of a speaker, and they enjoy providing and being provided for. They appreciate partners who let them take charge, but they also appreciate the security boundaries offer.

Advice for Taurus Sun-Capricorn Moon People:
- Remember to let people in and open up to others when you are feeling stressed.
- Be careful about how much you work. If you are not careful, you will become a workaholic.
- Be careful when working with other people. You can occasionally come across as pushy and overbearing.

Advice for Dealing with Taurus Sun-Capricorn Moon People:

- If a Taurus Sun-Capricorn Moon is stressed, ensure you do not leave them alone, as this can lead to them bottling up their emotions.
- Do not provoke these individuals as they can be very stubborn and occasionally quite nasty when crossed.
- They are hardworking and industrious. However, be careful that you do not take advantage of that as they will often do more than expected. Make sure the Taurus Sun-Capricorn Moon in your life takes breaks and focuses on themselves from time to time.

Capricorn Sun-Taurus Moon: The Gentle Critic

Capricorn Sun-Taurus Moon people are calm and eloquent and are determined to deal with their problems efficiently. They are realistic but have a positive outlook, and people find their advice about life's problems effective and reassuring. Their calm personality means their criticism is gentle but firm, and they offer a realistic judgment of the situation.

Good Traits: Uncomplaining, Determined, Persistent

These people have a dedicated mind and will never waste time complaining or feeling sorry for themselves. They work toward their goals with determination and will continue to work towards them even if life puts up obstacles in their way. They are ambitious and hardworking and make for good leaders and CEOs.

Bad Traits: Stubborn, Repressed, Rigid

While they work hard, sometimes this may devolve into stubbornness. They find it difficult to be flexible and adapt to changes in their life. They are also closed up and have difficulty expressing their emotions. This can lead to a buildup of negative emotions, eventually leading to an emotional outburst.

Perfect Partner: Capricorn Sun-Taurus Moon people appreciate the finer things in life and are looking for a partner who shares this appreciation. They want security and a stable partner, but their ambitious nature means they also want someone who improves their social status. Additionally, they need a partner who understands their way of doing things.

Advice for Capricorn Sun-Taurus Moon People:

- Remember to open up to people. A buildup of negative emotions will never go your way.
- Take time to have fun and relax. Your focus on success can lead to you forgetting to take downtime.
- Consider other options. Your lack of flexibility means you may lose out on opportunities, so look for ways to be more adaptable.

Advice for Dealing with Capricorn Sun-Taurus Moon People:

- If you are in a romantic relationship with a Capricorn Sun-Taurus Moon person, you may have to take the reins and be the spontaneous and imaginative one, as they are unlikely to take that role.
- Work with them and help them express their emotions. You should also be willing to open up simultaneously if you want to form a strong bond.
- When angered, these individuals can be ruthless, so it is best not to question their honesty or challenge their pride.

Capricorn Sun-Virgo Moon: The Reserved Scholar

These individuals tend to be shyer and more reserved than extroverted. They are rational and analytical and always work toward their goals with determination. They are skilled at grasping facts, which makes them suited for scholarly aims, and they do best when they have a single goal to focus on.

Good Traits: Logical, Practical, Loyal

Capricorn sun-Virgo moon people are great friends.

https://www.pexels.com/photo/anonymous-man-writing-on-chalkboard-near-group-of-diverse-students-at-table-6238020/

Capricorn Sun-Virgo Moon people are practical and down-to-earth. They do not waste time fantasizing and instead take action towards achieving their goals. At the same time, they are great friends and are always available to help when needed. They will not hesitate to complain about their issues but generally only need an ear to listen to them.

Bad Traits: Insecure, Self-Critical, Reserved

These individuals can be aloof and cautious, making them challenging to speak with. They are highly self-critical and insecure, and some of their cold and distant demeanor results from worries over the future. Their self-critical nature leads to a tendency to nervous disorders, always thinking of failures in place of successes.

Perfect Partner: Partners to Capricorn Sun-Virgo Moon individuals need to understand that work comes first for these individuals. They are devoted to their relationships and will always look for ways to help. To complement them, they need a neat and organized partner who understands that this sign is not the most romantic of individuals.

Advice for Capricorn Sun-Virgo Moon People:

- Take the time to be self-indulgent and focus on your successes instead of your failures. Without acknowledging your achievements, you will never be happy.
- Make sure that your focus on work does not become an obsession.
- Be willing to understand your partner's needs and focus on them instead of simply on work.

Advice for Dealing with Capricorn Sun-Virgo Moon People:

- These individuals appreciate being neat and organized, so ensure they are not surrounded by your clutter.
- Take the time to listen to them. These people are loyal and steadfast to their friends but require the same in return.
- These individuals can be picky and difficult to please, so you should know how to address their concerns without feeling bad or denigrating yourself.

Capricorn Sun-Capricorn Moon: The Serious Authoritarian

Double Capricorns are reserved and determined. Though they are not imposing, they can be too stubborn to take other opinions into account, giving them an authoritarian streak. At the same time, they are dependable; a double Capricorn's word is as good as gold.

Good Traits: Honest, Responsible, Dryly Witty

Double Capricorns are concerned with the facts. They are realistic and honest and not shallow in the least. They have been handling responsibilities since a young age, and it is something they enjoy. They also have a unique sense of humor that is both dry and sarcastic. While not everyone enjoys that, those who do enjoy their company.

Bad Traits: Distant, Ambitious, Controlling

These individuals are rarely satisfied with their achievements and always need more. This can lead to them becoming workaholics, and they need to open up and be more compassionate. Additionally, their inability to understand other opinions can lead to them becoming stubborn and, in some relationships, controlling.

Perfect Partner: The perfect partner to a double Capricorn will need to understand their need to be in charge. Additionally, they will need to understand that Capricorn Sun-Capricorn Moon individuals are reserved about their emotions and do not display them often. Double Capricorns need a partner who is not too needy and as ambitious as they are.

Advice for Capricorn Sun-Capricorn Moon People:

- Remember to open up to others and spend time socializing; otherwise, you risk becoming a workaholic.
- Understand that people often have different ideas and goals than your own.
- Open yourself to different perspectives to avoid becoming stubborn and defensive.

Advice for Dealing with Capricorn Sun-Capricorn Moon People:

- Double Capricorns have strong walls, but compliments can help you get past them, especially sincere ones.
- These individuals are afraid of getting hurt, making them seem cold and closed off. You will have to get them to trust you before they open up to you.
- Their desire for control means they often cannot see things from the right perspective. You will have to step in and act as a restraining influence on occasion.

Virgo Sun-Capricorn Moon: The Independent Realist

People with a Virgo-Capricorn Sun-Moon combination are independent individuals who dislike being restrained or controlled by others. They are also analytical and rational, able to set high goals and plan for the future and still approach things realistically. While their goals may be high, they are never impossible to reach.

Good Traits: Composed, Caring, Hardworking

These individuals are hardworking, dedicated to their goals, and motivated by success. They enjoy the limelight, and public recognition is important to them. At the same time, they are composed and caring in their personal relationships and are attentive to the needs of the people around them.

Bad Traits: Imposing, Distant, Erratic

When crossed, these individuals have a fearsome temper. Even though they think they are being composed, they can have volatile emotions they take out on the people around them. They do not understand people who are not as ambitious as they are and can even distance themselves from them. Additionally, while they try to be fair to others, their demeanor can be rude, imposing, and even tyrannical.

Perfect Partner: Virgo Sun-Capricorn Moon individuals need a partner with whom they can be their true selves. This includes understanding that, while they can be critical, it comes from a place of trying to help. They also need someone who can understand their need for independence, allowing them to retain it even in a romantic relationship.

Advice for Virgo Sun-Capricorn Moon People:

- Stay away from negative, pessimistic people. You will find it challenging to deal with them, leading to conflict.
- Be open to change, both at work and at home. Taking others' needs into account may be challenging, but it will improve your interpersonal relationships.
- Take the time to be open about your emotions with your partner. You can come across as closed off, which can

cause conflict in your relationship.

Advice for Dealing with Virgo Sun-Capricorn Moon People:

- Do not cross them. They have sharp tempers, and it is difficult to control them once they are angered.
- Keep an eye out for procrastination. If they are procrastinating, it is because they are not ready to start working, and you may need to intervene.
- They are looking for stable relationships and not short-term flings. If you get into a relationship with a Virgo Sun-Capricorn Moon, be prepared for things to get serious.

Virgo Sun-Taurus Moon: The Dependable Pragmatist

These individuals are solid and trustworthy with calm personalities. They rarely react emotionally unless under significant stress. They are patient and pragmatic, making them good managers and at business.

Good Traits: Loyal, Calm, Honest

Individuals with Virgo Sun-Taurus Moon are honest and own up to any mistakes they make. They can be relaxed and firm at the same time and are loyal in their relationships, both romantic and platonic.

Bad Traits: Judgmental, Eccentric, Reserved

These individuals think being sensitive and compassionate is a weakness. This can make them come across as both judgmental and reserved. They hide their emotions from everyone but their closest friends, and they dislike change. They can also be very erratic and difficult to deal with when stressed.

Perfect Partner: Virgo Sun-Taurus Moon individuals value security and look for that in a partner. Their perfect partner will be faithful and dependable like them but should be able to deal with their sometimes obsessive need for perfection.

Advice for Virgo Sun-Taurus Moon People:
- Open up to the people around you. While you do not have to, let them see as much as you show your closest loved ones, as being less reserved will help you make friends.
- Take the time to look at the bigger picture. If you do not, you may slip up without even realizing it.
- Do not fall for the misconception that compassion equals weakness. Take the time to understand the people with whom you are interacting.

Advice for Dealing with Virgo Sun-Taurus Moon People:
- They give great advice and are good people to consult when you need help.
- These individuals can fall into the trap of becoming complacent in their personal relationships. Do not take it personally; be prepared to shake them up if needed.
- They are not great with change, so if you hope to get them to try something new, be prepared to work for it.

Chapter 8: Sun-Moon Combinations II: Air Sun Signs

Have you ever wondered what it would be like to have the qualities of two different astrological signs? Suppose you are an air sign with your Sun in Gemini, Libra, or Aquarius and are interested in knowing more about your astrological personality. In that case, this is the chapter for you.

In this chapter, you will learn about the different Sun-Moon combinations and what each says about a person's personality. We will also look at the good and bad traits of each combination and the perfect partner for each one. Finally, we will give some advice on how to deal with each personality type.

Gemini Sun-Libra Moon: Social Butterfly

This combination is also known as the "social butterfly." People with this combination are known for their charm, wit, and intelligence. They are natural communicators and are always the life of the party. They are also very diplomatic and fair-minded and always see both sides of every issue.

Good Traits: Charismatic, Witty, Intelligent

If you were born with the Sun in Gemini and the Moon in Libra, you are a very social person who loves to communicate. You are also very fair-minded and have a strong sense of justice. You always want everyone to get along and are willing to compromise to maintain harmony.

Bad Traits: Indecisive, Gossips, Flirtatious

If you have a Gemini Sun and a Libra Moon, you might sometimes find yourself stuck between two different worlds. This can make it difficult for you to commit to anything, as you always second-guess yourself. You may also find yourself gossiping more than you should.

Perfect Partner: Gemini Sun-Aquarius Moon

Gemini Sun-Aquarius Moon is an excellent match for Gemini Sun-Libra Moon. These two signs share a strong intellectual connection and a love of freedom and independence. As long as they can respect each other's need for space, this relationship can be very fulfilling.

Advice for Gemini Sun-Libra Moon People:

If you have a Gemini Sun and a Libra Moon, here are some things to keep in mind:

- You need to balance your need for change and stability.
- Try not to be too indecisive. You need to learn to trust your instincts and make decisions quickly. Otherwise, you will miss out on opportunities.
- Stay loyal to your friends. They are the people who truly know and love you, and they will always be there for you.

Advice for Dealing with Gemini Sun-Libra Moon People:

If you are dealing with a Gemini Sun-Libra Moon person, here are some things to keep in mind:

- They are very social creatures, and if you want their attention, you need to be interesting.
- They are also very curious. Do not tell them if you do not want them to know something.
- Finally, they can be a bit flirty. If you are in a relationship with them, make sure to keep them in check.

Gemini Sun-Aquarius Moon: The Intellectual

This combination is also known as the "intellectual." People with this combination are known for their quick wit, intelligence, and originality. They are natural communicators and are always the life of the party. They are also very independent and have a strong need for freedom.

Good Traits: Quick-Witted, Original, Independent

If you have a Gemini Sun and an Aquarius Moon, you are probably one of the most quick-witted and intelligent people around. You are always coming up with new ideas and are not afraid to be different. You are also very independent and need your own space to grow and thrive.

Bad Traits: Detached, Arrogant, Unemotional

Those with this combination may find themselves being a bit detached from their emotions. You have difficulty understanding why people get so worked up about things, and you might find yourself withdrawing from emotional situations.

Perfect Partner: Cancer Sun-Pisces Moon

Cancer Sun-Pisces Moon is the perfect match for you as they will understand your need for space and freedom. In addition, they are very creative and imaginative, so you will always have something new and exciting to do together.

Advice for Gemini Sun-Aquarius Moon People:

If you have a Gemini Sun and an Aquarius Moon, here are some things to keep in mind:

- You need to find a balance between your intellectual side and your emotional side.
- Try not to be too detached from your emotions. You need to learn to understand and empathize with other people's feelings.
- Do not be a know-it-all. Sometimes, it is better to listen than to talk.

Advice for Dealing with Gemini Sun-Aquarius Moon People:

If you are dealing with a Gemini Sun-Aquarius Moon person, here are some things to keep in mind:

- They are very independent, so do not try to control them.
- They are also very intelligent. If you want their attention, you need to be interesting.
- Finally, they can be a bit unemotional. Do not take everything they say or do personally.

Libra Sun-Gemini Moon: The Communicator

This combination is also known as the "communicator." People with this combination are known for their communication skills, social nature, and ability to see sides of every issue. They are natural diplomats and are always able to find common ground.

Good Traits: Social, Diplomatic, Balanced

If you have a Libra Sun and a Gemini Moon, you are probably one of the most social and diplomatic people around. You are always able to find common ground, and you are very good at mediation. You are also very balanced and fair-minded and always see both sides of every issue.

Bad Traits: Indecisive, People-Pleasing, Superficial

Those with this combination might find themselves being a bit too indecisive. In addition, you can be a bit of a people-pleaser, and you may need to learn to stand up for yourself. You may also be superficial because you are so good at diplomacy that you never seem to take a firm stand on anything.

Perfect Partner: Aries Sun-Capricorn Moon

Aries Sun-Capricorn Moon is the perfect match for you as they will be able to help you with your indecision. They are also very independent and strong-willed, so you will never have to worry about them trying to control you. In addition, they are very down-to-earth and practical, so you will always have someone to rely on.

Advice for Libra Sun-Gemini Moon People:

If you have a Libra Sun and a Gemini Moon, here are some things to keep in mind:

- You need to find a balance between your social side and your more introverted side.
- You need to learn to make decisions. Indecision can be a real problem for you.
- You also need to learn to stand up for yourself. Do not be a doormat.

Advice for Dealing with Libra Sun-Gemini Moon People:

If you are dealing with a Libra Sun-Gemini Moon person, here are some things to keep in mind:

- They need their space. Do not try to force them into anything they do not want to do.
- They are very independent. Do not try to control them.
- They can be a bit indecisive. You must be interesting and make things happen if you want their attention.

Gemini Sun-Gemini Moon: The Chameleon

This combination is also known as the "chameleon." People with this combination are known for their adaptability, versatility, and resourcefulness. They are natural communicators and are always the life of the party. They are also very independent and have a strong need for freedom.

Good Traits: Adaptable, Resourceful, Versatile

If you have a Gemini Sun and a Gemini Moon, you are probably one of the most adaptable and resourceful people around. You can always find new solutions to problems and are not afraid to try new things. You are also very independent and need your own space to grow and thrive.

Bad Traits: Scattered, Inconsistent, Flaky

Those with this combination may find themselves being a bit scattered and inconsistent. You may have difficulty sticking to one thing for a long time, and you may find yourself changing your mind a lot. You also need a lot of freedom, so you might not do well in situations where you feel trapped.

Perfect Partner: Aries Sun-Aquarius Moon

Aries Sun-Aquarius Moon is the perfect match for you as they are also adaptable and independent. They are not afraid of change and will always be up for trying new things. In addition, they are very spontaneous and exciting, so you will never be bored when you are with them.

Advice for Gemini Sun-Gemini Moon People:

If you have a Gemini Sun and a Gemini Moon, here are some things to keep in mind:

- Find a balance between your need for freedom and your need for stability.
- Try not to be too scattered. Focus on one thing at a time and see it through to the end.
- Do not be afraid to try new things. Life is full of surprises, so embrace them!
- Finally, be flexible. Things will always change, so learn to go with the flow.

Advice for Dealing with Gemini Sun-Gemini Moon People:

If you are dealing with a Gemini Sun-Gemini Moon person, here are some things to keep in mind:

- They are very adaptable and resourceful, so they can usually find a way to get what they want.
- They need their freedom, so do not try to control them.
- They can be a bit scattered and inconsistent so try to be patient with them.

Libra Sun-Aquarius Moon: The Visionary

Libra Sun and Aquarius Moon are highly creative and visionary combinations. You are drawn to the arts and have a strong sense of intuition. You see the world in terms of potential and possibilities and are always searching for new ways to express yourself.

Good Traits: Creative, Visionary, Intuitive

If you have a Libra Sun and an Aquarius Moon, you are probably one of the most creative and visionary people around. You are always searching for new ways to express yourself, and you have a strong sense of intuition. You are always seeking knowledge and understanding and are not afraid to challenge conventional thinking.

Bad Traits: Scattered, Disconnected, Unpredictable

The downside of this combination is that you can sometimes be seen as scattered or disconnected. You may have trouble finishing things, and you can be very unpredictable. You may also find it difficult to relate to people, as you always see the world differently.

Perfect Partner: Gemini Sun-Aquarius Moon

If you are a Libra Sun and Aquarius Moon, your perfect partner is a Gemini Sun and Aquarius Moon. This combination is the perfect match for your creative and visionary nature. In addition, you will always have someone who understands your need for freedom and independence.

Advice for Libra Sun-Aquarius Moon People:

If you have a Libra Sun and an Aquarius Moon, here are some things to keep in mind:

- You need to learn to focus your energy and use your creative power for good.
- You need to find a way to express your unique perspective to the world.
- You also need to learn to be more organized and focused. Indecision can be a real problem for you.

Advice for Dealing with Libra Sun-Aquarius Moon People:

If you are dealing with a Libra Sun and Aquarius Moon person, here are some things to keep in mind:

- Be patient with them. They might take a while to make up their mind.
- Encourage them to express their unique perspective. It is one of their greatest strengths.
- Finally, do not try to control them. They need their freedom and independence, so let them be.

Libra Sun-Libra Moon: The Idealist

This combination is known as the "idealist." People with this combination are known for their idealism, compassion, and diplomacy. They are natural peacemakers who are always looking for ways to unite people. They are also very fair-minded and have a strong sense of justice.

Good Traits: Idealistic, Compassionate, Diplomatic

If you have a Libra Sun and a Libra Moon, you are probably one of the most idealistic and compassionate people around. You are always looking for ways to help others and are very quick to forgive. You are also very fair-minded and always see both sides of every issue.

Bad Traits: Indecisive, Manipulative, Gullible

Those with this combination might find themselves being a bit indecisive and manipulative. You may have a hard time making decisions, and you may find yourself trying to control others. You also tend to be very gullible and can be easily taken advantage of.

Perfect Partner: Gemini Sun-Aquarius Moon

Gemini Sun-Aquarius Moon is the perfect match for you as they are also idealistic and independent. They are not afraid of change and will always be up for trying new things. In addition, they are very spontaneous and exciting, so you will never be bored when you are with them.

Advice for Libra Sun-Libra Moon People:

If you have a Libra Sun and a Libra Moon, here are some things to keep in mind:

- Try to be more decisive. Indecision can lead to missed opportunities.
- Do not try to control others. Everyone has a path to follow.
- Be wary of people who try to take advantage of your gullibility.

Advice for Dealing with Libra Sun-Libra Moon People:

If you are dealing with a Libra Sun-Libra Moon person, here are some things to keep in mind:

- They are very idealistic and compassionate, so they might not be realistic.
- They need their freedom, so do not try to control them.
- They can be a bit indecisive and manipulative, so try to be patient with them.

Aquarius Sun-Gemini Moon: The Thinker

Aquarius Suns with Gemini Moons are known for their quick wit and intelligence. They are natural-born leaders with a sharp mind for strategy. But they are not just all talk; these folks are also *doers*. When they set their sights on something, they go after it with determination and tenacity.

Good Traits: Intelligent, Leader, Innovative

People with an Aquarius Sun and Gemini Moon are some of the most intelligent and innovative people around. They are always searching for new knowledge and have a strong desire to make a difference in the world. They are natural-born leaders who are always looking for new ways to grow and express themselves.

Bad Traits: Scattered, Impatient, Unpredictable

The downside of this combination is that you can sometimes be seen as scattered or disconnected. You may have trouble finishing things, and you can be very unpredictable. You may also find it difficult to relate to people, as you always see the world differently.

Perfect Partner: Aries Sun-Gemini Moon

If you are an Aquarius Sun and Gemini Moon, your perfect partner is an Aries Sun and Gemini Moon. This combination is the perfect match for your intelligence and drive. You will always have someone who understands your need for freedom and independence. In addition, you will never get bored, as your partner is always full of new ideas and energy.

Advice for Aquarius Sun-Gemini Moon People:

If you have an Aquarius Sun and Gemini Moon, here are some things to keep in mind:

- Focus your energy and use your intelligence for good.

- Find a way to express your unique perspective to the world.
- Organize your thoughts and be more focused. Indecision can be a real problem for you.

Advice for Dealing with Aquarius Sun-Gemini Moon People:

If you are dealing with an Aquarius Sun and Gemini Moon person, here are some things to keep in mind:

- Keep an open mind. They are always searching for knowledge and new perspectives.
- Encourage them to express their unique ideas. It is one of their greatest strengths.
- Finally, do not try to control them. They need their freedom and independence, so let them be.

Aquarius Sun-Libra Moon: The Idealist

Individuals with this Sun-Moon combination are hardworking idealists who strive for balance and harmony. People born under this influence are natural peacemakers and mediators, always looking for ways to bring people together. Overall, those with an Aquarius Sun and Libra Moon are kindhearted souls who work tirelessly to make the world a better place.

Good Traits: Altruistic, Mediator, Idealistic

If you have an Aquarius Sun and Libra Moon, you are probably a very altruistic and idealistic person. You always strive for balance and harmony and are quick to lend a listening ear or a helping hand. In addition, you are probably a very hardworking person looking for ways to improve the world.

Bad Traits: People-Pleaser, Indecisive, Overly Idealistic

The downside of this combination is that you can sometimes be seen as a people-pleaser. You may have trouble making decisions as you always try to find the best solution for everyone. In addition, some people may see you as too idealistic.

Perfect Partner: Gemini Sun-Libra Moon

If you are an Aquarius Sun and Libra Moon, your perfect partner is a Gemini Sun and Libra Moon. This combination is the perfect match for your altruism and idealism. You will always have someone who understands your need for balance and harmony. In addition, you will never get bored, as your partner is always full of new ideas and energy.

Advice for Aquarius Sun-Libra Moon People:

If you have an Aquarius Sun and Libra Moon, here are some things to keep in mind:

- Do not try to please everyone. Focus on what is best for you and your partner.
- Make decisions based on logic, not emotion.
- Be careful of being too idealistic. It can sometimes lead to unrealistic expectations.

Advice for Dealing with Aquarius Sun-Libra Moon People:

If you are dealing with an Aquarius Sun and Libra Moon person, here are some things to keep in mind:

- Do not try to change them. They are who they are and will never try to be someone they are not.
- Encourage their idealism. It is one of their greatest strengths.
- Be patient with them. They may take longer than others to make decisions, but they always try to find the best solution for everyone involved.

Now that you know about the different Sun-Moon combinations, you should better understand the different personalities out there. Remember, this is just a general guide. Not everyone will fit perfectly into one of these categories. The most important thing is to be yourself and to find someone who accepts you for who you are.

Chapter 9: Sun-Moon Combinations III: Water Sun Signs

Water Sun signs are often described as being "in their feelings." If you have a water Sun sign such as Pisces, Cancer, or Scorpio, you may find that you are especially tuned in to the emotional energies of those around you.

If you have a water Sun sign and a water Moon sign, this chapter will explore some of the potential traits and qualities you may possess. It will also provide insight into how to use your emotional sensitivity to your advantage.

Pisces Sun-Scorpio Moon: The Intense Idealist

The combination of Pisces Sun and Scorpio Moon creates an intense, idealistic, and compassionate individual. Those with this combination are often deeply in touch with their emotions and may find themselves drawn to helping others. They may also be highly intuitive and have a strong connection to the spiritual realm.

Good Traits: Passionate, Loyal, Intuitive, Spiritual

Pisces Sun-Scorpio Moon individuals are often passionate about their beliefs and very loyal to those they care about. They may also be highly intuitive and strongly connected to the spiritual realm. With their intense emotions, they understand and relate to others on a deep level.

Bad Traits: Distracted, Secretive, Jealous, Possessive

Pisces Sun-Scorpio Moon combinations tend to be easily distracted.
https://unsplash.com/photos/BNrlDv8w07Y?utm_source=unsplash&utm_medium=referral&utm_content=creditShareLink

Pisces Sun and Scorpio Moon individuals can be easily distracted, and their imaginations can sometimes run wild. They can also be quite secretive and often have a dark side they may not show to others. They may have a dark side that they do not show to others and are often drawn to the mysterious and the unusual.

Perfect Partner: Taurus Sun-Cancer Moon

The perfect partner for the Pisces Sun-Scorpio Moon is the Taurus Sun-Cancer Moon. This pairing is ideal because they share similar emotional needs and desires. Both signs are loyal, compassionate, and protective of those they love. They will also understand and support each other on a deep level.

Advice for Pisces Sun-Scorpio Moon:

If you have a Pisces Sun-Scorpio Moon, here are some tips that may help you make the most of your combination:

- Try to stay focused and ground yourself in reality.
- Be careful not to get too caught up in your own emotions.
- Don't be afraid to express your emotions.
- Be honest with yourself and others.
- Try to stay calm and centered on your emotions.

Advice for Dealing with Pisces Sun-Scorpio Moon:

If you know a Pisces Sun-Scorpio Moon, here are some tips that may help you deal with them:

- Be patient with them.
- Try to be understanding and compassionate.
- Do not try to control or manipulate them.
- Be honest with them.
- Allow them to express their emotions.

Pisces Sun-Cancer Moon: The Nurturing Mystic

The Pisces Sun-Cancer Moon is a unique and special combination. Those with this combination are often very intuitive and in touch with their emotions. They are also deeply compassionate and caring, always ready to lend a shoulder to cry on. If you know someone with this combination, consider yourself lucky. You have a true friend for life.

Good Traits: Caring, Nurturing, Compassionate

Pisces Sun-Cancer Moon individuals strongly connect to the spiritual world and often possess psychic abilities. This combination gives them a natural ability to nurture and care for others. They are gentle healers who often go out of their way to help those in need.

Bad Traits: Needy, Moody, clingy

Pisces Sun-Cancer Moon individuals may occasionally come across as needy or clingy. They may also be quite moody, and their emotions can sometimes get the best of them. However, these individuals are usually well-meaning and just need some understanding and compassion.

Perfect Partner: Virgo Sun-Capricorn Moon

The perfect partner for the Pisces Sun-Cancer Moon is the Virgo Sun-Capricorn Moon. This pairing is ideal because they share similar emotional needs and desires. Both signs are loyal, compassionate, and protective of those they love. They will also understand and support each other on a deep level.

Advice for Pisces Sun-Cancer Moon:

If you have a Pisces Sun-Cancer Moon, here are some tips that may help you make the most of this combination:

- Try to stay in touch with your emotions.
- Don't be afraid to express your feelings.
- Be patient with yourself and others.
- Try to stay calm and centered.
- Allow yourself to be nurtured and cared for.

Advice for Dealing with Pisces Sun-Cancer Moon:

If you know a Pisces Sun-Cancer Moon, here are some tips that may help you deal with them:

- Let them know that you are there for them.
- Be understanding and compassionate.
- Encourage them to express their emotions.
- Respect their need for space and privacy.

Pisces Sun-Pisces Moon: The Compassionate Dreamer

Pisces is the gentle dreamer of the zodiac, and those with a Pisces Sun and Pisces Moon are especially in tune with their emotions and intuition. Pisces are natural healers, and their ability to connect with others on a soul level is what makes them so special. If you know Pisces, be sure to cherish them, as they are truly one of a kind.

Good Traits: Compassionate, Intuitive, Caring

Pisces Sun-Pisces Moon individuals are some of the most compassionate and caring people you will ever meet. They are also highly intuitive and in touch with their emotions. Pisces have a natural ability to heal and comfort others, and they are often drawn to professions that involve helping others, like counseling or social work.

Bad Traits: Overly Sensitive, Moody, Escapist

Pisces Sun-Pisces Moon individuals may occasionally come across as overly sensitive or moody. They may have a tendency to escape from their problems instead of facing them head-on. However, these individuals are usually well-meaning and just need a little extra understanding and compassion.

Perfect Partner: Cancer Sun-Scorpio Moon

The perfect partner for the Pisces Sun-Pisces Moon is the Cancer Sun-Scorpio Moon. This pairing is ideal because they share similar emotional needs and desires. Both signs are loyal, compassionate, and protective of those they love.

Advice for Pisces Sun-Pisces Moon:

If you have a Pisces Sun-Pisces Moon, here are some tips that may help you make the most of your combination:

- Channel your compassionate and intuitive nature into helping others.
- Create a safe and comfortable space for yourself to relax and dream.
- Get in touch with your emotions and allow yourself to feel them fully.
- Do not be afraid to express your feelings.

Advice for Dealing with Pisces Sun-Pisces Moon:

If you know a Pisces Sun-Pisces Moon, here are some tips that may help you deal with them:

- Look for ways to help them channel their compassionate and intuitive nature.
- Give them space to relax and dream.
- Encourage them to get in touch with their emotions.
- Respect their need for privacy and solitude.

Cancer Sun-Pisces Moon: The Sensitive Homebody

Cancer is the nurturing homebody of the zodiac, and those with a Cancer Sun and Pisces Moon are especially sensitive and in touch with their emotions. Cancer is a natural caregiver, and their ability to create a warm and loving home is what makes them so special. If you know Cancer, make sure you cherish them, as they are truly one of a kind.

Good Traits: Sensitive, Nurturing, Caring

Cancer Sun-Pisces Moon individuals are some of the most sensitive and nurturing people you will ever meet. They have a natural ability to care for others, and their homes are usually warm and inviting. Cancer is loyal and protective of those they love, and they often make excellent parents.

Bad Traits: Overly Sensitive, Moody, clingy

Cancer Sun-Pisces Moon individuals may occasionally come across as overly sensitive or moody. They may also have a tendency to be clingy or needy at times. However, these individuals are usually well-meaning and just need a little extra understanding and compassion.

Perfect Partner: Virgo Sun-Taurus Moon

The perfect partner for the Cancer Sun-Pisces Moon is the Virgo Sun-Taurus Moon. This pairing is ideal because they share similar emotional needs and desires. Both signs are loyal, reliable, and patient. They also have a shared love of security and stability.

Advice for Cancer Sun-Pisces Moon:

If you have a Cancer Sun-Pisces Moon, here are some tips that may help you make the most of your combination:

- Channel your nurturing nature into caring for others.
- Create a warm and inviting home that is a haven from the outside world.
- Get in touch with your emotions and allow yourself to feel them fully.
- Do not be afraid to express your feelings.

Advice for Dealing with Cancer Sun-Pisces Moon:

If you know a Cancer Sun-Pisces Moon, here are some tips that may help you deal with them:

- Look for ways to help them channel their nurturing nature.
- Give them space to relax and dream.
- Encourage them to get in touch with their emotions.
- Respect their need for privacy and solitude.

Cancer Sun-Scorpio Moon: The Sensual Survivor

Cancer Sun-Scorpio Moon is a potent and passionate combination. Those with this combination are highly sensitive and have a strong intuitive connection to the emotions of others. They are also natural survivors who can overcome any obstacle. Cancer is loyal and protective of those they love, and they often make excellent parents.

Good Traits: Sensitive, Intuitive, Passionate

Cancer Sun-Scorpio Moon individuals are some of the most sensitive and intuitive people you will ever meet. They have a strong connection to the emotions of others, and they can use this knowledge to their advantage. They are also passionate and intense. They are natural survivors.

Bad Traits: Jealous, Possessive, Manipulative

Cancer Sun-Scorpio Moon individuals may occasionally come across as jealous or possessive. They may also tend to be manipulative or controlling at times. However, they are usually well-meaning and just need some understanding and compassion.

Perfect Partner: Pisces Sun-Cancer Moon

The perfect partner for the Cancer Sun-Scorpio Moon is the Pisces Sun-Cancer Moon. This pairing is ideal because they share similar emotional needs and desires. Both signs are loyal, reliable, and patient. They also have a shared love of security and stability.

Advice for Cancer Sun-Scorpio Moon:

If you have a Cancer Sun-Scorpio Moon, here are some tips that may help you make the most of your combination:

- Channel your intuitive nature into understanding the emotions of others.
- Use your passion to drive you toward your goals.
- Never give up, no matter how hard things get.
- Allow yourself to be vulnerable with those you trust.

Advice for Dealing with Cancer Sun-Scorpio Moon:

If you know a Cancer Sun-Scorpio Moon, here are some tips that may help you deal with them:

- Encourage them to channel their intuitive nature into something positive.
- Help them to find an outlet for their passion.
- Be there for them when they need someone to lean on.
- Respect their need for privacy and solitude.

Cancer Sun-Cancer Moon: The Emotional Caretaker

Cancer Sun-Cancer Moon is a deeply emotional and compassionate combination. Those with this combination are natural caretakers who are always there for the people they love. They are also highly intuitive and have a strong connection to their emotions. Cancer is loyal and protective of those they love, and they often make excellent parents.

Good Traits: Emotional, Compassionate, Intuitive

Cancer Sun-Cancer Moon individuals are some of the most emotional and compassionate people you will ever meet. They strongly connect to their emotions and are always there for the people they love. They are also highly intuitive and have a strong sense of intuition.

Bad Traits: Overly Sensitive, Moody, Possessive

Cancer Sun-Cancer Moon individuals may occasionally come across as overly sensitive or moody. They may also tend to be possessive at times. However, these individuals are usually well-meaning and just need some understanding and compassion.

Perfect Partner: Pisces Sun-Pisces Moon

The perfect partner for the Cancer Sun-Cancer Moon is the Pisces Sun-Pisces Moon. This pairing is ideal because they share similar emotional needs and desires. Both signs are loyal, reliable, and patient. They also have a shared love of security and stability.

Advice for Cancer Sun-Cancer Moon:

If you have a Cancer Sun-Cancer Moon, here are some tips that may help you make the most of this combination:

- Use your emotional nature to your advantage.
- Take care of yourself so you can be there for the people you love.
- Make sure to nurture your relationships.
- Allow yourself to be vulnerable with those you trust.

Advice for Dealing with Cancer Sun-Cancer Moon:

If you know a Cancer Sun-Cancer Moon, here are some tips that may help you deal with them:

- Let them know that you appreciate their emotional nature.
- Encourage them to take care of themselves.
- Make sure to nurture your relationship.

Scorpio Sun-Cancer Moon: The Passionate Protector

Scorpio Sun-Cancer Moon is a passionate and compassionate combination. Those with this combination are natural protectors who are always there for the people they love. They are also highly intuitive and have a strong connection to their emotions. Scorpio Sun-Cancer Moon individuals often make excellent parents.

Good Traits: Passionate, Compassionate, Intuitive

Scorpio Sun-Cancer Moon individuals are some of the most passionate and compassionate people you will ever meet. They strongly connect to their emotions and are always there for the people they love. Scorpio Sun-Cancer Moon also has a strong sense of intuition.

Bad Traits: Overly Sensitive, Moody, Jealous

Scorpio Sun-Cancer Moon individuals may occasionally come across as overly sensitive or moody. They may also tend to be jealous at times. However, these individuals are usually well-meaning and just need some understanding and compassion.

Perfect Partner: Pisces Sun-Pisces Moon

The perfect partner for the Scorpio Sun-Cancer Moon is the Pisces Sun-Pisces Moon. This pairing is ideal because they share similar emotional needs and desires. Both signs are loyal, reliable, and patient. They also have a shared love of security and stability.

Advice for Scorpio Sun-Cancer Moon:

If you have a Scorpio Sun-Cancer Moon, here are some tips that may help you make the most of your combination:

- Break out of your comfort zone and try new things.
- Prepare for the worst but hope for the best.
- Take your time when making decisions.
- Learn to trust your intuition.

Advice for Dealing with Scorpio Sun-Cancer Moon:

If you know a Scorpio Sun-Cancer Moon, here are some tips that may help you deal with them:

- Appreciate their passion and compassion.
- Encourage them to take care of themselves.
- Make sure to nurture your relationship.

Scorpio Sun-Pisces Moon: The Jealous Lover

Scorpio Sun and Pisces Moon are a great match. These two signs are both associated with water, making for a very emotional and intense connection. Scorpio is known for being jealous and possessive, but Pisces is also very loyal and devoted. This can create a very intense and passionate relationship, as both partners will be extremely committed to one another.

Good Traits: Passionate, Loyal, Devoted

Scorpio Sun-Pisces Moon individuals are some of the most passionate and loyal people you will ever meet. They are also very devoted to the people they love. Scorpio Sun-Pisces Moon individuals often make excellent parents.

Bad Traits: Jealous, Possessive, Overly Sensitive

Scorpio Sun-Pisces Moon individuals may occasionally come across as jealous or possessive. They may also have a tendency to be overly sensitive at times. However, these individuals are usually well-meaning and just need some understanding and compassion.

Perfect Partner: Cancer Sun-Cancer Moon

The perfect partner for the Scorpio Sun-Pisces Moon is the Cancer Sun-Cancer Moon. This pairing is ideal because they share similar emotional needs and desires. Both signs are loyal, reliable, and patient. They also have a shared love of security and stability.

Advice for Scorpio Sun-Pisces Moon:

If you have a Scorpio Sun-Pisces Moon, here are some tips that may help you make the most out of this combination:

- Create a safe and secure environment for yourself and your loved ones.
- Do not let your emotions overwhelm you.
- Try to be patient with yourself and others.
- Learn to trust your intuition.

Advice for Dealing with Scorpio Sun-Pisces Moon:

If you know a Scorpio Sun-Pisces Moon, here are some tips that may help you deal with them:

- Appreciate their passion and loyalty.
- Encourage them to take care of themselves.
- Make sure to nurture your relationship.

Scorpio Sun-Scorpio Moon: The Intense Investigator

People with a Scorpio Sun and Scorpio Moon are one of the most intense combinations. They are the detectives of the zodiac, always probing and looking for answers. They feel deeply, and their emotions run high. They can be quite dramatic at times.

Good Traits: Sharp, Passionate, Resourceful

Scorpio Sun-Scorpio Moon individuals are some of the sharpest and most resourceful people you will ever meet. They are also very passionate and can be quite persuasive when they want to be. They have a sharp intellect and are not afraid to use it.

Bad Traits: Jealous, Possessive, Controlling

Scorpio Sun-Scorpio Moon individuals may occasionally come across as jealous or possessive. They may also have a tendency to be controlling at times. However, these individuals are usually well-meaning and just need some understanding and compassion.

Perfect Partner: Cancer Sun-Cancer Moon

The perfect partner for the Scorpio Sun-Scorpio Moon is the Cancer Sun-Cancer Moon. The emotions of these two signs are in sync. When one is happy, the other is happy. When one is sad, the other is sad. They understand each other's need for security and stability. It is a very nurturing and supportive relationship.

Advice for Scorpio Sun-Scorpio Moon:

If you have a Scorpio Sun-Scorpio Moon, here are some tips that may help you make the most of your combination:

- Get to know yourself and your emotions.
- Learn to control your emotions.
- Be honest with yourself and others.
- Find a partner who understands you.

Advice for Dealing with Scorpio Sun-Scorpio Moon:

If you know a Scorpio Sun-Scorpio Moon, here are some tips that may help you deal with them:

- Appreciate their passion and intensity.
- Encourage them to get to know themselves.
- Make sure to nurture your relationship.

Each Sun-Moon combination is unique and has its own set of strengths and weaknesses. This chapter has only scratched the surface. To really understand yourself or someone else, it is important to look at the whole chart. However, the Sun-Moon combination is a good place to start. Look up your combination and see what it has to say about you.

Chapter 10: Sun-Moon Combinations IV: Fire Sun Signs

Now that we have covered the Sun-Moon combinations for the earth, air, and water signs, the next step is to look at the fire signs. If your sign is Aries, Leo, or Sagittarius, your Sun sign is a fire sign. In this chapter, we will take a look at the different Sun-Moon combinations, including each option's good and bad traits. We will also figure out the perfect partner for you and offer advice you can use for yourself or when interacting with an individual who belongs to one of these signs.

Aries Sun-Aries Moon: The Charismatic Visionary

Dual Aries have truly magnetic personalities. They can fiercely express themselves when needed. Intelligent and brilliant, they are driven by a need to be challenged at all times and are interested in change. A lack of change will leave them bored, and they are the type to be drawn to subjects like science, medicine, and social studies. Their minds are always busy, making them effective leaders.

Positive Traits: Action Oriented, Responsible, Multifaceted

These individuals need to have a range of hobbies to keep them busy. They are always ready to act when needed but will also never express an opinion unless they are certain of the veracity of their words. Full of energy, they invest much effort into each situation.

Negative Traits: Blunt, Impatient, Egocentric

These individuals express their opinions freely, which can be positive, but it can also result in causing harm to people around them. Additionally, they cannot understand other perspectives and consider what they need. To be satisfied, they need things to keep moving or risk boredom. Additionally, they are reckless, and they react to the slightest provocation.

Perfect Partner: Dual Aries individuals need someone who will always challenge them. At the same time, their perfect partner should be a calming influence on their dynamic and energetic nature, and they get along well romantically with Taurus Moons. Dual Aries individuals are too egoistic to be involved in a long-distance relationship. They need events to happen in the here and now, and long-distance relationships do not afford them that.

Advice for Aries Sun-Aries Moon People:

- Remember to set attainable goals. You tend to chase after moon-shot dreams to the detriment of the people around you.
- Take the time to understand people around you. Your focus on yourself can affect your interpersonal relationships.
- Think things through. Being too reckless can easily backfire on you.

Advice for Dealing with Aries Sun-Aries Moon People:

- Try not to provoke or cross them. They can be reckless and volatile when tested.
- They like to fight for the people they love, so give them a challenge and a reason to fight.
- Take time to work with them. They are huge individualists, and it will take some time before they are willing to open up to you and see both of you as a singular team.

Aries Sun-Leo Moon: The Exuberant Egotist

These individuals are highly energetic and magnetic. They love interacting with people and have a deep desire for social interaction. They enjoy the limelight and know how to showcase themselves in the most flattering light. At the same time, they can be stuck in their ways and hate giving up control to others.

Good Traits: Imaginative, Affectionate, and Sociable

They love interacting with people and are warm and generous. They are moved by the suffering of others and will always be the first to share their time and resources to help others. While stuck in their ways, they also have great, innovative ideas, which will see them become successful.

Bad Traits: Trusting, Impulsive, Attention-Seeking

Their desire for social interaction shows them developing a histrionic, attention-seeking personality to the point where they become captives to their own vanity. They lack good judgment and may fall prey to those with negative intentions. They easily get into relationships but never know how to end them well.

Perfect Partner: Aries Sun-Leo Moons need someone who admires them and is happy to take care of them. They get bored easily, so you must keep them entertained. They also need attention as being ignored will result in unhappiness. When in the right relationship, however, they are generous and devoted romantics who are great at long-term relationships when motivated to do so.

Advice for Aries Sun-Leo Moon People:

- Look for ways to stay interested when you feel your attention slipping, or else you may miss out on important moments
- Consider other options. Being stuck in your way may lead to you missing out on better solutions
- While cynicism is not something to aim for, being slightly wary about strangers' comments will serve you well

Advice for Dealing with Aries Sun-Leo Moon People:

- Keep an eye out for them to ensure they do not get scammed. As mentioned above, their intuition is not the

best.
- When they are successful, make sure to admire and celebrate them, as their desire for public accolades is quite high.
- In frustrating situations, they can be impatient and short-tempered, so make sure you have solutions ready before breaking bad news to them.

Aries Sun-Sagittarius Moon: The Philosopher

Patient, thoughtful, and determined, these individuals have a philosophical approach to life and will never take action for no reason. They are strident believers in the truth and are led by their personal ideals. They have a wanderlust driven by the desire to find out what life is really about.

Good Traits: Independent, Enthusiastic, Determined

Aries Sun-Sagittarius Moon will never give up once they have decided on a course of action. Their enthusiastic, dynamic personality means they love challenges and living in the moment. They enjoy being in charge and making decisions for themselves instead of on behalf of others.

Bad Traits: Authoritative, Impulsive, Stubborn

Their dynamism also means that they do not think through their decisions. While each action has a reason, it is not necessarily well-reasoned, which can get them into trouble. Additionally, while they are independent, their desire for control can make them authoritative and autocratic.

Perfect Partner: The perfect partner for these individuals is as passionate about life as they are and will be direct and open with them. Their way of expressing themselves may occasionally veer into the hurtful, so their partners should have thick skins. Their desire for travel means they seek out sociable people who will travel with them.

Advice for Aries Sun-Sagittarius Moon People:
- Consider giving others a bit of control. This will improve your interpersonal relationships and allows you to get to know different perspectives
- Make sure you are patient and thoughtful and fight impulsivity and agitation.
- Train yourself not to fall for generalizations and snap judgments.

Advice for Dealing with Aries Sun-Sagittarius Moon People:
- Variety is the spice of their lives, so constant change and the opportunity for new discoveries are a must to keep them interested.
- They are straightforward and see things in black and white, so be ready for direct, frank conversations.
- You will need to help them understand others' perspectives, emotions, and opinions, as they can often be self-absorbed and forget about those around them.

Leo Sun-Aries Moon: The Alpha

These individuals are extremely forthright in their opinions. They can come across as aggressive but are also highly esteemed, and their opinion is greatly valued. They are born leaders and need to be in control of things to be truly happy.

Good Traits: Passionate, Confident, Productive

When a Leo Sun-Aries Moon sets their mind on something, they will achieve it. These individuals need to be involved in everything happening, and they will fight for people and causes that they think are worthwhile. Their enthusiasm means they burn brightly and turn their aggression into productivity.

Bad Traits: Aggressive, Controlling, Self-Centered

These individuals love the limelight and enjoy attention from others. If they decide they deserve something, they will work to get it, to the detriment of others. Their leadership skills can often manifest as aggression and overt control, while their reactive nature means they often act without thinking.

Perfect Partner: These individuals need a partner who challenges them every step of the way. Their perfect other half needs to be honest and trustworthy and able to shower them with the praise they crave. They desire passion and excitement in their lives and look for it in the people they enter into romantic relationships with.

Advice for Leo Sun-Aries Moon People:

- Remember to think of others. Letting your emotions rule you can turn you into a selfish person lacking in empathy, which can affect your interpersonal relationships.
- Be humble about your successes. Making waves in the world is an achievement, but refraining from crowing about it will bring you more respect.
- Remember to listen to and incorporate the advice of others in your life.

Advice for Dealing with Leo Sun-Aries Moon People:

- Try not to take their bluntness to heart. They are like this with everyone, and their bluntness comes from a place of kindness.
- Appreciate them for their successes. Verbal affirmations are essential for their happiness.
- Be prepared for the risk of emotional tantrums, as these are simply signs that they fully trust you.

Leo Sun-Leo Moon: The Noble Leader

Focused and determined, dual Leos are self-controlled natural-born leaders. They are willing to fight for themselves and others and can be compassionate and warm when in charge. They enjoy attention and admiration and can be jealous, possessive, insecure, and authoritarian without it.

Good Traits: Friendly, Generous, Charismatic

These individuals are cheerful and good-natured and get along well with people while still retaining their independent streak. They are generous and easygoing in their friendships, and their strong charisma means that people flock to them and their good nature.

Bad Traits: Authoritarian, Ruthless, Vain

A dual Leo's vanity can only be satisfied with admiration and praise from the people around them. Their natural leadership tendencies can occasionally become authoritarian, damaging their personal relationships. When crossed, they are absolutely ruthless in their response.

Perfect Partner: These individuals need a partner to give them the attention they crave. They need to be the center of the world for the people around them, but especially for their other half. The more they feel they are important to their partner, the more attention they will pay to them in gifts, romantic gestures, and time.

Advice for Leo Sun-Leo Moon People:

- Look for measures of success beyond the material.
- Though you are social, take care when choosing who your inner circle of friends and confidants is.
- Remember to bring yourself to the level of the people around you. Acting as if you are in charge when around friends can result in broken friendships and bitterness.

Advice for Dealing with Leo Sun-Leo Moon People:

- More than anything, these individuals need to be showered with attention. The more you give them, the closer they will be to you.
- They can be jealous and possessive in romantic relationships, so their partners should know how to react.
- Do not cross them. They treat anyone they see as enemies ruthlessly, and you will never be able to develop any relationship (let alone a friendship) with a dual Leo once you provoke them.

Leo Sun-Sagittarius Moon: Bluntly Independent

These individuals are extremely straightforward and honest, to the point of bluntness. They do not mind that speaking the truth can make them unpopular; they will still say what is on their minds. They are extremely independent and are unhappy when tied down or restricted from doing as they please.

Good Traits: Principled, Passionate, Caring

They are highly passionate and enthusiastic about meeting their goals and succeeding in life. They are charming, energetic, have a vivid imagination, and believe strongly in honesty and truth. They look to inspire others, and while they can be blunt, they are also well-intentioned.

Bad Traits: Flighty, Selfish, Restless

These individuals are often motivated by inspiration instead of hard work, making it challenging for them to stick to a single job or relationship. They are impatient and always looking for a change and are extremely restless when they feel tied down or at the beck and call of others.

Perfect Partner: Their perfect partner should love change and adventure and should love to travel as much as these individuals do. They also need constant attention. Lack of it can result in them losing interest, so their perfect partner should be willing to provide enough of it. Additionally, their other half should be okay with their honesty, as being unable to express themselves can be stifling.

Advice for Leo Sun-Sagittarius Moon People:

- Look for ways to constructively channel your passion for achieving great things.
- Be patient with others, and keep their potential reaction to your words in mind before being blunt.
- While your optimism is a strong trait, temper it with a dose of realism, or you risk becoming reckless.

Advice for Dealing with Leo Sun-Sagittarius Moon People:

- Give them the attention they crave. If they feel ignored, they will turn their attention away from you.
- They can find patience challenging, so you may have to be patient with them instead.
- Try not to give them too many orders as this can make them unhappy and tied down.

Sagittarius Sun-Aries Moon: The Adventurer

Freedom-loving, honest, and outspoken, these individuals love adventure and are always on the lookout for action and excitement. They love to be challenged and often cannot stay in one place for long. However, this can also lead them to act on impulse instead of thinking things through.

Good Traits: Intelligent, Humorous, Charming

These individuals are great at satire and make brilliant comedians. Their humor and positivity make them charming and, combined with their energetic personality, make people constantly drawn to them. Despite their occasionally reckless nature, they are also extremely intelligent and can be very profound when speaking to others, and it is their inquisitive mind that pushes them to constantly seek new challenges.

Bad Traits: Reckless, Restless, Impulsive

Their desire for adventure and challenges means they find it difficult to stay in one place for long. As soon as they learn something new, they need to have an opportunity to put it into practice. Their courageous and adventurous nature means they are always looking for further excitement, which can make them careless and reckless.

Perfect Partner: Their perfect partner will be someone who is patient with them as they can often forget to listen to their other half's needs. At the same time, their easygoing nature means their partner should be ambitious and give them the push they may need to go ahead with their plans. Though they have a temper and fiery personalities, they do not hold grudges. Because of this, their other half should be calm. A partner who loves arguing can bring out the worst in them.

Advice for Sagittarius Sun-Aries Moon People:

- Remember to give your partner the attention they need and let them occasionally take charge.
- While your direct nature is part of your charm, not everyone will appreciate it.

- Take the time to think your decisions through before you make them. If you do not, you risk making a major mistake.

Advice for Dealing with Sagittarius Sun-Aries Moon People:
- Their love for satire can occasionally lead to them making fun of the people around them, and you should be direct with them if you are uncomfortable with this.
- They can be insensitive in their personal life but expect a lot of attention in turn. Again, being direct with your feelings will help.
- Their positivity can result in them seeming a bit naive. However, they are unaware of the dark side and simply choose to look at the best parts of life.

Sagittarius Sun-Leo Moon: The Honorable Intellectual

People with this sign constantly pursue the mysteries and knowledge of the universe. At the same time, they value tolerance and honor, and once they give their word, they will not break it. They give their reputation a lot of importance and treat everyone with integrity and kindness.

Good Traits: Curious, Friendly, Energetic

These individuals are constantly searching for more information and are always willing to share this knowledge with others. Their eagerness and honesty make them great friends, and when their idealistic nature and desire to help are channeled properly, they can be great leaders.

Bad Traits: Vain, Stubborn, High-Maintenance

Sagittarius Sun-Leo Moon individuals love being in the spotlight and must be told they are special. They enjoy the attention, which can make them appear vain and high-maintenance, especially in their personal relationships. They are also extremely stubborn, and they dislike accepting advice or admitting they made a mistake.

Perfect Partner: Their perfect partner must understand that their easy-going nature comes with a constant desire to achieve more in life. They need someone who sets goals that are as lofty as theirs, someone who is always willing to attempt the impossible. They also need a partner who gives them the appreciation they crave, which can take the form of attention, gifts, time, or all of them together.

Advice for Sagittarius Sun-Leo Moon People:

- Your love for humanity will make you extremely successful in the social service field, and it is where you will find happiness.
- Remember to take the time to appreciate others just as they appreciate you.
- Be flexible and listen to the advice offered to you. What you do with it is your decision.

Advice for Dealing with Sagittarius Sun-Leo Moon People:

- Give them the attention they crave. Without it, they can become extremely dramatic.
- Remember that, while their honesty and integrity are praiseworthy, they are still human. Many see them as perfect people, and placing them on a pedestal can sometimes bring out the worst in them.
- Do not try to convince them that something is impossible. As far as they are concerned, *impossible* does not exist.

Conclusion

In this book, you have learned that your zodiac sign can indicate much more than just potential prospects for your future. Once you master the language of astrology, you will be able to reveal the secrets behind the stars, namely, how they affect your birth chart. Along with the four cardinal elements, the astrological planets exert enormous power over each zodiac sign. Each planet transits between the signs, and the one ruling over a sign at the time you were born will determine your core personality. The Sun and the Moon have the most prominent influence. The Sun determines your outer personality and can help you reveal how your inner light shines over the different areas of your life, whereas the Moon defines your soul's desires, wants, and needs – which you often hide from the outside world. Since the Sun does not move, its energy is distributed over the rest of the astrological planets, anchoring them and guiding them through the zodiac signs. Your journey toward discovering your personality starts by revealing your Sun sign.

That being said, the fine traits of your personality will always come from the energy zodiac sign present on your birth chart. Each sign is influenced by one of the four cardinal elements and their qualities. According to the element they are ruled by, the 12-star signs are divided into four triplicities, which are Fire signs, Water signs, Air signs, and Earth signs. These are further split into quadruplicities defined by the quality associated with the element at the time you were born. Quadruplicities change seasonally and typically indicate how stable specific personality traits were in the season you were born. The energy of the star signs manifests differently in each zodiac house, further narrowing down how it will influence your personality traits.

So, essentially, your entire personality is determined by the combination of your Sun sign, Moon sign, zodiac sign, and the element that influences the latter. Each group of combinations (the Earth-Sun-Moon signs, the Water-Sun-Moon signs, the Fire-Sun-Moon signs, and the Air-Sun-Moon signs) carries a set of unique personality traits. While your zodiac sign can reveal your positive and negative traits, the Sun-Moon combination can help you define these further. This will allow you to understand your emotions, thoughts, and actions more. It can also enable you to understand people born under a particular star combination and connect with them despite the differences in your personalities. Last, but not least, it will help you find people with similar combinations and perhaps reveal your ideal partner.

Here's another book by Silvia Hill that you might like

Free Bonus from Silvia Hill available for limited time

Hi Spirituality Lovers!

My name is Silvia Hill, and first off, I want to THANK YOU for reading my book.

Now you have a chance to join my exclusive spirituality email list so you can get the ebooks below for free as well as the potential to get more spirituality ebooks for free! Simply click the link below to join.

P.S. Remember that it's 100% free to join the list.

~~$27~~ FREE BONUSES

- 9 Types of Spirit Guides and How to Connect to Them
- How to Develop Your Intuition: 7 Secrets for Psychic Development and Tarot Reading
- Tarot Reading Secrets for Love, Career, and General Messages

Access your free bonuses here
https://livetolearn.lpages.co/sun-signs-paperback/

References

Rose, E. (2022, May 2). Sun Sign Meaning: What It Says About You & Who You're Destined To Become. StyleCaster. https://stylecaster.com/sun-sign-meaning/

Blanchfield, T. (2022, February 15). The psychology behind why we care about astrology. Verywell Mind. https://www.verywellmind.com/the-psychology-behind-why-we-care-about-astrology-5217929

Brown, M. (2021, August 11). What is astrology? A beginners' guide to the language of the sky. InStyle. https://www.instyle.com/lifestyle/astrology/what-is-astrology

Coughlin, S. (2022, May 3). How to make sense of your birth chart. Refinery29. https://www.refinery29.com/en-us/2016/11/129929/birth-chart-analysis-natal-astrology-reading

Definition of ASTROLOGY. (n.d.). Merriam-Webster.Com. https://www.merriam-webster.com/dictionary/astrology

Delgado, C. (2021, August 24). Why are people so into astrology right now? Discover Magazine. https://www.discovermagazine.com/mind/why-are-people-so-into-astrology-all-of-a-sudden

Grabianowski, E. (2005, May 26). What is astrology? HowStuffWorks. https://entertainment.howstuffworks.com/horoscopes-astrology/question749.htm

How to interpret your Birth Chart. (n.d.). Tree of Life. https://treeoflife.com.au/blogs/news/how-to-interpret-your-birth-chart

Mahtani, N. (2020, March 31). Your astrology birth chart reveals more than you might expect. Nylon. https://www.nylon.com/astrology-birth-chart

Sloan, E. (2021, July 13). Here's What Each Planet Actually Means in Astrology—So You Can Understand Your Chart in More Depth. Well+Good. https://www.wellandgood.com/meanings-of-planets-in-astrology/

Astrology Planets and their Meanings, Planet Symbols and Cheat Sheet. (2018, January 27). Labyrinthos. https://labyrinthos.co/blogs/astrology-horoscope-zodiac-signs/astrology-planets-and-their-meanings-planet-symbols-and-cheat-sheet

Thomas, K. (2021, November 5). A guide to the planets in astrology and what they each represent. New York Post. https://nypost.com/article/astrology-planets-meaning/

Solar System Symbols. (n.d.). NASA Solar System Exploration. https://solarsystem.nasa.gov/resources/680/solar-system-symbols

Atkinson, N. (2015, November 25). Order Of the Planets From The Sun. Universe Today. https://www.universetoday.com/72305/order-of-the-planets-from-the-sun/

Brown, M., & Kassel, G. (2021, January 22). The Need-to-Know Traits and Qualities of Every Single Zodiac Sign. Shape. https://www.shape.com/lifestyle/mind-and-body/zodiac-signs-meanings-dates

Stapleton, D. (2020, April 2). Aries Zodiac Sign: Characteristics, Dates, & More. Astrology.Com. https://www.astrology.com/zodiac-signs/aries

Stapleton, D. (2020, April 29). Taurus Zodiac Sign: Characteristics, Dates, & More. Astrology.Com. https://www.astrology.com/zodiac-signs/taurus

Stapleton, D. (2020, April 13). Gemini Zodiac Sign: Characteristics, Dates, & More. Astrology.Com. https://www.astrology.com/zodiac-signs/gemini

Stapleton, D. (2020, March 11). Cancer Zodiac Sign: Characteristics, Dates, & More. Astrology.Com. https://www.astrology.com/zodiac-signs/cancer

Stapleton, D. (2020, April 6). Leo Zodiac Sign: Characteristics, Dates, & More. Astrology.Com. https://www.astrology.com/zodiac-signs/leo

Stapleton, D. (2020, April 30). Virgo Zodiac Sign: Characteristics, Dates, & More. Astrology.Com. https://www.astrology.com/zodiac-signs/virgo

Stapleton, D. (2020, April 14). Libra Zodiac Sign: Characteristics, Dates, & More. Astrology.Com. https://www.astrology.com/zodiac-signs/libra

Stapleton, D. (2020, May 14). Scorpio Zodiac Sign: Characteristics, Dates, & More. Astrology.Com. https://www.astrology.com/zodiac-signs/scorpio

Stapleton, D. (2020, April 6). Sagittarius Zodiac Sign: Characteristics, Dates, & More. Astrology.Com. https://www.astrology.com/zodiac-signs/sagittarius

Stapleton, D. (2020, February 29). Capricorn Zodiac Sign: Characteristics, Dates, & More. Astrology.Com. https://www.astrology.com/zodiac-signs/capricorn

Stapleton, D. (2020, April 16). Aquarius Zodiac Sign: Characteristics, Dates, & More. Astrology.Com. https://www.astrology.com/zodiac-signs/aquarius

Houses. (n.d.). Astrology.com. https://www.astrology.com/houses

The 12 houses of astrology - the astrological houses and your natal chart. (2020, August 14). Labyrinthos. https://labyrinthos.co/blogs/astrology-horoscope-zodiac-signs/the-12-houses-of-astrology-the-astrological-houses-and-your-natal-chart

Alicia. (2015, March 18). 7 challenging Taurus traits and how to overcome them. All Women's Talk. https://inspiration.allwomenstalk.com/challenging-taurus-traits-and-how-to-overcome-them/

Aries 101: Everything you need to know about the Kickstarter of the zodiac. (2021, March 26). Mindbodygreen. https://www.mindbodygreen.com/articles/aries-sign-101

Astrology Zodiac Signs. (n.d.-a). Aquarius Zodiac Sign: Horoscope, dates, Traits & personality. Astrology-Zodiac-Signs.Com. https://www.astrology-zodiac-signs.com/zodiac-signs/aquarius/

Astrology Zodiac Signs. (n.d.-b). Leo Zodiac Sign: Horoscope, dates, Traits & personality. Astrology-Zodiac-Signs.Com. https://www.astrology-zodiac-signs.com/zodiac-signs/leo/

Astrology Zodiac Signs. (n.d.-c). Libra Zodiac Sign: Horoscope, dates, Traits & personality. Astrology-Zodiac-Signs.Com. https://www.astrology-zodiac-signs.com/zodiac-signs/libra/

Astrology Zodiac Signs. (n.d.-d). Pisces Zodiac Sign: Horoscope, dates, Traits & personality. Astrology-Zodiac-Signs.Com. http://astrology-zodiac-signs.com/zodiac-signs/pisces/

Astrology Zodiac Signs. (n.d.-e). Scorpio Zodiac Sign: Horoscope, dates, Traits & personality. Astrology-Zodiac-Signs.Com. https://www.astrology-zodiac-signs.com/zodiac-signs/scorpio/

Astrology Zodiac Signs. (n.d.-f). Virgo Zodiac Sign: Horoscope, dates, traits & personality. Astrology-Zodiac-Signs.Com. https://www.astrology-zodiac-signs.com/zodiac-signs/virgo/

Brown, M. (2020a, March 13). Your Aries zodiac sign guide: Everything to know about the fierce fire sign. InStyle. https://www.instyle.com/lifestyle/astrology/aries-zodiac-sign

Brown, M. (2020b, April 3). Your Taurus zodiac sign guide: Everything to know about the sensual earth sign. InStyle. https://www.instyle.com/lifestyle/taurus-zodiac-sign

Brown, M. (2020c, April 17). Your Gemini zodiac sign guide: Everything to know about the curious air sign. InStyle. https://www.instyle.com/lifestyle/gemini-zodiac-sign

Brown, M. (2020d, May 11). Your Cancer zodiac sign guide: Everything to know about the heartfelt water sign. InStyle. https://www.instyle.com/lifestyle/cancer-zodiac-sign

Brown, M. (2020e, May 28). Your Leo zodiac sign guide: Everything to know about the spotlight-loving fire sign. InStyle. https://www.instyle.com/lifestyle/leo-zodiac-sign

Brown, M. (2020f, June 19). Your Virgo zodiac sign guide: Everything to know about the detail-oriented earth sign. InStyle. https://www.instyle.com/lifestyle/virgo-zodiac-sign

Brown, M. (2020g, June 30). Your Libra zodiac sign guide: Everything to know about the social butterfly air sign. InStyle. https://www.instyle.com/lifestyle/libra-zodiac-sign

Brown, M. (2020h, July 23). Scorpio zodiac sign: Everything to know about the magnetic water sign. InStyle. https://www.instyle.com/lifestyle/scorpio-zodiac-sign

Brown, M. (2020i, August 3). Your Sagittarius zodiac sign guide: Everything to know about the adventurous fire sign. InStyle. https://www.instyle.com/lifestyle/sagittarius-zodiac-sign

Brown, M. (2020j, August 20). Your Capricorn zodiac sign guide: Everything to know about the motivated earth sign. InStyle. https://www.instyle.com/lifestyle/capricorn-zodiac-sign

Brown, M. (2020k, August 28). Your Aquarius zodiac sign guide: Everything to know about the quirky air sign. InStyle. https://www.instyle.com/lifestyle/aquarius-zodiac-sign

Brown, M. (2020l, September 8). Your Pisces zodiac sign guide: Everything to know about the dreamy water sign. InStyle. https://www.instyle.com/lifestyle/pisces-zodiac-sign

Crowley, R. (2018, July 28). If you have something to say about "B*tchy" Virgos, read this first. POPSUGAR. https://www.popsugar.com/love/Best-Qualities-Virgos-45069076

Everything to know about Taurus, the zodiac's stubborn-but-loving sign. (2021, May 4). Mindbodygreen. https://www.mindbodygreen.com/articles/taurus-101-personality-traits-compatability-and-more

Everything you need to know about the zodiac's most eclectic sign. (2022, January 17). Mindbodygreen. https://www.mindbodygreen.com/articles/aquarius

Garis, M. G. (2022, March 17). 6 Aries personality traits that sum up what it means to live life horns-first. Well+Good. https://www.wellandgood.com/aries-personality-traits/

Hrdlitschka, S. (2005). Sun Signs. Orca Book. https://www.astroyogi.com/zodiac-signs/sunsigns

Iwegbue, A., & Smith, E. W. (2020, April 9). 40 celeb Cancers who do their zodiac sign proud. Cosmopolitan. https://www.cosmopolitan.com/entertainment/celebs/g32086359/famous-cancer-celebrities/

Kelly, A. (2018a, February 2). Libra zodiac sign: Personality traits and sign dates. Allure. https://www.allure.com/story/libra-zodiac-sign-personality-traits

Kelly, A. (2018b, February 2). Pisces zodiac sign: Personality traits and sign dates. Allure. https://www.allure.com/story/pisces-zodiac-sign-personality-traits

Kelly, A. (2018c, February 2). Scorpio zodiac sign: Personality traits and sign dates. Allure. https://www.allure.com/story/scorpio-zodiac-sign-personality-traits

Kelly, A. (2018d, February 2). The personality of a Cancer, explained. Allure. https://www.allure.com/story/cancer-zodiac-sign-personality-traits

Kelly, A. (2018e, February 2). The personality of a Capricorn, explained. Allure. https://www.allure.com/story/capricorn-zodiac-sign-personality-traits

Kelly, A. (2018f, February 2). The personality of a Gemini, explained. Allure. https://www.allure.com/story/gemini-zodiac-sign-personality-traits

Kelly, A. (2018g, February 2). The personality of a Leo, explained. Allure. https://www.allure.com/story/leo-zodiac-sign-personality-traits

Kelly, A. (2018h, February 2). The personality of a Taurus, explained. Allure. https://www.allure.com/story/taurus-zodiac-sign-personality-traits

Kelly, A. (2018i, February 2). The personality of a Virgo, explained. Allure. https://www.allure.com/story/virgo-zodiac-sign-personality-traits

Kelly, A. (2018j, February 2). The personality of an Aries, explained. Allure. https://www.allure.com/story/aries-zodiac-sign-personality-traits

Kelly, A. (2018k, February 2). The personality traits of a Sagittarius, including their compatibility with other signs. Allure. https://www.allure.com/story/sagittarius-zodiac-sign-personality-traits

Lapik, E. (2020a, April 13). 25 positive & Negative Virgo Personality Traits and characteristics. Astromix.Net / Blog. https://astromix.net/blog/virgo-traits/

Lapik, E. (2020b, April 16). 19 positive & negative Aquarius personality traits and characteristics. Astromix.Net / Blog. https://astromix.net/blog/aquarius-traits/

Lapik, E. (2020c, May 7). Positive & negative Sagittarius personality traits and characteristics. Astromix.Net / Blog. https://astromix.net/blog/sagittarius-traits/

Lapik, E. (2020d, May 10). 20 positive & negative Gemini personality traits and characteristics. Astromix.Net / Blog. https://astromix.net/blog/gemini-traits/

Lapik, E. (2020e, May 13). 20 positive & negative Aries personality traits and characteristics. Astromix.Net / Blog. https://astromix.net/blog/aries-traits/

Lapik, E. (2020f, May 13). 20 positive & negative Cancer personality traits and characteristics. Astromix.Net / Blog. https://astromix.net/blog/cancer-traits/

Lapik, E. (2020g, May 13). 22 positive & negative Taurus personality traits and characteristics. Astromix.Net / Blog. https://astromix.net/blog/taurus-traits/

Lapik, E. (2020h, June 12). 20 positive & negative Capricorn personality traits and characteristics. Astromix.Net / Blog. https://astromix.net/blog/capricorn-traits/

Lapik, E. (2020i, June 12). 20 positive & negative Pisces personality traits and characteristics. Astromix.Net / Blog. https://astromix.net/blog/pisces-traits/

Lapik, E. (2020j, June 14). 20 positive & negative Libra personality traits and characteristics. Astromix.Net / Blog. https://astromix.net/blog/libra-traits/

Lapik, E. (2020k, June 14). 25 positive & negative Leo personality traits and characteristics. Astromix.Net / Blog. https://astromix.net/blog/leo-traits/

Leo compatibility: What to know about dating or befriending this sign. (2021, July 23). Mindbodygreen. https://www.mindbodygreen.com/articles/leo-sign-101

Meet Cancer: The nurturing & emotional water sign of the zodiac. (2021, June 22). Mindbodygreen. https://www.mindbodygreen.com/articles/cancer-sign-101

Meet Gemini: The wise & witty air sign of the zodiac. (2021, June 2). Mindbodygreen. https://www.mindbodygreen.com/articles/gemini-sign-101

Meet Pisces: The go-with-the-flow psychic of the zodiac. (2021, March 12). Mindbodygreen. https://www.mindbodygreen.com/articles/pisces-sign-101

Meet Virgo: The zodiac's most dependable & detail-oriented sign. (2021, August 24). Mindbodygreen. https://www.mindbodygreen.com/articles/virgo-sign-101

Merinuk, M. (2022, May 26). Gemini celebrities: Which of your favorite stars are born under the sign of the twins? TODAY. https://www.today.com/life/astrology/gemini-celebrities-rcna23436

Mulroy, C. (2022, April 21). Taurus celebrities: Which of your favorite stars are born under the sign of the bull? TODAY. https://www.today.com/life/astrology/taurus-celebrities-rcna24439

Pai, R. (2021, September 22). 15 bad traits and characteristics of A Sagittarius (man & woman). MomJunction. https://www.momjunction.com/articles/negative-traits-of-a-sagittarius_00771750/

Scorpio sign 101: Personality traits, compatibility & more. (2021, October 24). Mindbodygreen. https://www.mindbodygreen.com/articles/scorpio

Smith, E. W. (2020a, May 26). 40 celebs who prove Leos belong in the spotlight. Cosmopolitan. https://www.cosmopolitan.com/lifestyle/g32671448/famous-leo-celebrities/

Smith, E. W. (2020b, June 10). These famous Virgos will make you wish you were one too. Cosmopolitan. https://www.cosmopolitan.com/entertainment/celebs/g32803997/famous-virgo-celebrities/

Smith, E. W. (2020c, July 28). 40 celebs who prove Libras were born to be famous. Cosmopolitan. https://www.cosmopolitan.com/entertainment/g33445883/famous-libra-celebrities/

Smith, E. W. (2020d, August 17). 40 Scorpio celebrities who prove they're the most intense sign. Cosmopolitan. https://www.cosmopolitan.com/lifestyle/g33627026/famous-scorpio-celebrities/

Smith, E. W. (2020e, September 10). 40 celebrities who are total Sagittariuses. Cosmopolitan. https://www.cosmopolitan.com/entertainment/celebs/g33983622/famous-sagittarius-celebrities/

Smith, E. W. (2020f, October 7). 40 celebs who prove Capricorns really are the greatest. Cosmopolitan. https://www.cosmopolitan.com/entertainment/celebs/g34303556/famous-capricorn-celebrities/

Smith, E. W. (2020g, November 23). 25 Aquarius celebrities who are just like their sun sign. Cosmopolitan. https://www.cosmopolitan.com/entertainment/celebs/g34759491/famous-aquarius-celebrities/

Sullivan, C., & Smith, E. W. (2021, January 21). These 31 celebrities are total Aries. Cosmopolitan. https://www.cosmopolitan.com/entertainment/celebs/g35217933/famous-aries-celebrities/

Tenorio, I. (2020, September 21). Why Are Aries so difficult? YourTango. https://www.yourtango.com/2020336922/why-are-aries-so-difficult

The Editors of Encyclopedia Britannica. (2021). zodiac. In Encyclopedia Britannica.

The zodiac's most thrill-seeking sign—and the secret to winning them over. (2021, November 21). Mindbodygreen. https://www.mindbodygreen.com/articles/sagittarius

This sign is the "boss" of the zodiac—but it's often misunderstood. (2021, December 20). Mindbodygreen. https://www.mindbodygreen.com/articles/capricorn

Thomas, K. (2022, March 18). Aries celebrities: 25 famous people born under the sign of the ram. New York Post. https://nypost.com/article/aries-celebrities-25-famous-people-born-under-zodiac-sign/

TIMESOFINDIA.COM. (2021, February 3). Your core purpose in life, according to all zodiac signs. Times of India. https://timesofindia.indiatimes.com/life-style/relationships/love-sex/your-core-purpose-in-life-according-to-all-zodiac-signs/photostory/80650045.cms?picid=80650200

What does your sun, moon, and rising sign really mean? (n.d.). Mindbody. https://explore.mindbodyonline.com/blog/wellness/what-does-your-sun-moon-and-rising-sign-really-mean

Your ultimate guide to zodiac's most ethical & equitable sign. (2021, September 22). Mindbodygreen. https://www.mindbodygreen.com/articles/libra-sign-101

(N.d.). Symbolspy.Com. https://www.symbolspy.com/zodiac-symbols-text.html

Angel, J. (2015, April 6). What's your emotional mode of operation? Harper's BAZAAR. https://www.harpersbazaar.com/horoscopes/a10491/whats-your-emotional-mode-of-operation/

Astrology: Moon in the signs. (2015, April 18). Cafeastrology.Com; Cafe Astrology .com. https://cafeastrology.com/articles/mooninsigns_pg2.html

Brown, M. (2020, September 25). What your moon sign means about your personality and life path. Shape. https://www.shape.com/lifestyle/mind-and-body/moon-sign-meaning

Daruwalla, C. B. (2022, May 17). Sun Sign Vs Moon Sign: What is it and which is better? India TV. https://www.indiatvnews.com/astrology/sun-sign-vs-moon-sign-which-is-better-zodiac-signs-latest-astrology-news-2022-05-17-777252

DeVille, A. (2019, June 10). Your natal moon: A powerful asset in workplace relationships. Llewellyn Worldwide. https://www.llewellyn.com/journal/article/2760

Douglas, M. (n.d.). Cancer moon sign: Personality and relationships. Prepscholar.Com. https://blog.prepscholar.com/cancer-moon-sign

Elara, L. (n.d.). Moon in Aries: 6 strengths & 5 weaknesses of the Natal moon in Aries. https://popularastrology.com/aries-moon

Gemsyogi, W. by. (2019, August 5). Taurus moon sign - personality, positive & negative traits. GemsYogi. https://gemsyogi.com/taurus-moon-sign/

Hall, M. (2007a, February 26). Personality traits of an Aries moon sign. LiveAbout. https://www.liveabout.com/moon-in-aries-moon-signs-206981

Hall, M. (2007b, March 4). Scorpio moon sign: Personality and characteristics. LiveAbout. https://www.liveabout.com/scorpio-moon-moon-signs-206988

Hall, M. (2007c, March 4). What are Traits of the Libra Moon Person? LiveAbout. https://www.liveabout.com/moon-in-libra-moon-signs-206985

Hall, M. (2007d, March 13). Pisces moon sign: Personality and characteristics. LiveAbout. https://www.liveabout.com/moon-in-pisces-206986

Kelly, Alice. (2022a, March 4). What it means if you were born under A Gemini moon sign. YourTango. https://www.yourtango.com/zodiac/gemini-moon-sign

Kelly, Alice. (2022b, March 9). What it means if you were born under A Capricorn moon. YourTango. https://www.yourtango.com/zodiac/capricorn-moon-sign

Kelly, Alice. (2022c, March 9). What it means if you were born under A Sagittarius Moon. YourTango. https://www.yourtango.com/zodiac/sagittarius-moon-sign

Kelly, Alice. (2022d, March 10). What it means if you were born under A Cancer moon. YourTango. https://www.yourtango.com/zodiac/cancer-moon-sign

Kelly, Alice. (2022e, March 11). What it means if you were born under A Scorpio moon. YourTango. https://www.yourtango.com/zodiac/scorpio-moon-sign

Kelly, Aliza. (2018, April 23). What your moon sign says about your emotional personality. Allure. https://www.allure.com/story/zodiac-moon-sign-emotional-personality

Montúfar, N. (2022a, March 21). Everything you need to know about that Aries Moon in your birth chart. Cosmopolitan. https://www.cosmopolitan.com/lifestyle/a39490505/aries-moon-meaning/

Montúfar, N. (2022b, May 20). If your moon sign is cancer, here's what astrology says about you. Cosmopolitan. https://www.cosmopolitan.com/lifestyle/a40061764/cancer-moon-meaning/

Moon in Gemini. (2021, March 23). MyPandit. https://www.mypandit.com/zodiac-signs/gemini/moon-in-gemini/

Moon in Scorpio celebrities who live intensely. (n.d.). Horoscope.Com https://www.horoscope.com/us/editorial/editorial-news.aspx?UniqueID=1952&CRC=CCC6EFE73F6169A915ECD36BBD17E2E7

Moon in Taurus. (2021, March 19). MyPandit. https://www.mypandit.com/zodiac-signs/taurus/moon-in-taurus/

Moon in the signs: Astrology. (2015, April 18). Cafeastrology.Com; Cafe Astrology .com. https://cafeastrology.com/articles/mooninsigns.html

Moon signs - know your moon sign/Rashi according to your birth time - Surat Diamond. (n.d.). Suratdiamond.Com
https://www.suratdiamond.com/moonsigns.aspx

Painter, S., & More, R. (n.d.). Moon in Gemini signs show bright, engaging personality traits. LoveToKnow.
https://horoscopes.lovetoknow.com/astrology-signs-personality/moon-gemini-signs-show-bright-engaging-personality-traits

Punarvasu, P. (n.d.). For Libra moon signs, is banking and finance a wise career option. Indastro. from https://www.indastro.com/astrology-articles/career-in-banking-and-finance-for-libra-moon-sign.html

Robinson, A. (n.d.). Capricorn moon sign: What you should know. Prepscholar.Com. https://blog.prepscholar.com/capricorn-moon-sign

Rose, K. (2022, March 16). What it means if you were born under an Aries Moon. YourTango. https://www.yourtango.com/zodiac/aries-moon-sign

Ruby, M. (2021a, October 28). Celebrities with Virgo moon. Ranker. https://www.ranker.com/list/virgo-moon-celebrities/madame-ruby?page=2

Ruby, M. (2021b, November 8). Celebrities with Capricorn moon. Ranker. https://www.ranker.com/list/celebrities-with-capricorn-moon/madame-ruby

Ruby, M. (2021c, November 12). Taurus moon celebrities. Ranker. https://www.ranker.com/list/taurus-moon-celebrities/madame-ruby

Ruby, M. (2021d, November 15). Gemini moon celebrities. Ranker. https://www.ranker.com/list/gemini-moon-celebrities/madame-ruby

Ruby, M. (2021e, December 6). Celebrities with Leo moon. Ranker. https://www.ranker.com/list/leo-moon-celebrities/madame-ruby

Ruby, M. (2021f, December 6). Moon in Sagittarius celebrities. Ranker. http://ranker.com/list/moon-in-sagittarius-celebrities/madame-ruby

Stardust, L. (2021, February 24). Are you passionate? Impulsive? This is what your moon sign says about your emotional personality. Vogue India. https://www.vogue.in/culture-and-living/content/what-your-moon-sign-says-about-your-emotional-personality-zodiac-signs

The best profession for energetic Aries. (n.d.). Indastro. https://www.indastro.com/aries/best-profession-aries.html

Your moon sign is the last piece of the astrology puzzle, so here's what it means. (2021, October 20). ELLE. https://www.elle.com.au/culture/moon-sign-meaning-26111

Denise. (2018a, September 3). Capricorn Sun Capricorn Moon: A venturesome personality. I.TheHoroscope.Co. https://i.thehoroscope.co/capricorn-sun-capricorn-moon-a-venturesome-personality/

Denise. (2018b, September 3). Capricorn Sun Taurus Moon: A stoic personality. I.TheHoroscope.Co. https://i.thehoroscope.co/capricorn-sun-taurus-moon-a-stoic-personality/

Denise. (2018c, September 25). Virgo Sun Capricorn Moon: A rational personality. I.Tthe horoscope.Co. https://i.thehoroscope.co/virgo-sun-capricorn-moon-a-rational-personality/

Denise. (2018d, September 25). Virgo Sun Taurus Moon: A composed personality. I. TheHoroscope.Co. https://i.thehoroscope.co/virgo-sun-taurus-moon-a-composed-personality/

Denise. (2018e, October 14). Taurus Sun Capricorn Moon: A practical personality. I. TheHoroscope.Co. https://i.thehoroscope.co/taurus-sun-capricorn-moon-a-practical-personality/

Denise. (2018f, October 14). Taurus Sun Taurus Moon: A benevolent personality. I. TheHoroscope.Co. https://i.thehoroscope.co/taurus-sun-taurus-moon-a-benevolent-personality/

Denise. (2018g, October 14). Taurus Sun Virgo Moon: A brilliant personality. I. TheHoroscope.Co. https://i.thehoroscope.co/taurus-sun-virgo-moon-a-brilliant-personality/

Facebook, H. F., Iii. (2011, January 24). Astrology Western Sun and Moon sign combinations. Hugh Fox III. https://foxhugh.com/divination/sun-and-moon-sign-combinations/

Moon, J. (2017, November 23). Sun-Moon astrology combinations. Astroligion.com. https://astroligion.com/sun-moon-astrology-combinations/

Moon, J. (2018a, October 11). Virgo sun Taurus moon personality. Astroligion.com. https://astroligion.com/virgo-sun-taurus-moon/

Moon, J. (2018b, October 14). Virgo sun Capricorn moon personality. Astroligion.com. https://astroligion.com/virgo-sun-capricorn-moon/

Moon, J. (2018c, October 28). Capricorn sun Taurus moon personality. Astroligion.com. https://astroligion.com/capricorn-sun-taurus-moon/

Moon, J. (2018d, October 28). Capricorn sun Virgo moon personality. Astroligion.com. https://astroligion.com/capricorn-sun-virgo-moon/

Moon, J. (2019a, March 13). Taurus Sun Capricorn Moon Personality. Astroligion.com. https://astroligion.com/taurus-sun-capricorn-moon-personality/

Moon, J. (2019b, March 13). Taurus Sun Taurus Moon personality. Astroligion.com. https://astroligion.com/taurus-sun-taurus-moon-personality/

Moon, J. (2019c, March 13). Taurus Sun Virgo Moon personality. Astroligion.com. https://astroligion.com/taurus-sun-virgo-moon-personality/

Sesay, A. (2020, November 18). Balancing the light and dark: Understanding your sun and moon in astrology. Byrdie. https://www.byrdie.com/astrology-sun-and-moon-5086414

Stardust, L. (2022, March 11). Earth signs will inspire you with their groundedness. Cosmopolitan. https://www.cosmopolitan.com/lifestyle/a33588028/earth-signs-astrology

Sun in Capricorn & moon in signs. (n.d.). I. TheHoroscope.Co. https://i.thehoroscope.co/astrology/sun-moon/sun-in-capricorn/

Sun in Taurus & moon in signs. (n.d.). I. TheHoroscope.Co. https://i.thehoroscope.co/astrology/sun-moon/sun-in-taurus/

Sun in Virgo & moon in signs. (n.d.). I. TheHoroscope.Co. https://i.thehoroscope.co/astrology/sun-moon/sun-in-virgo/

Facebook, H. F., Iii. (2011, January 24). Astrology Western Sun and Moon sign combinations. Hugh Fox III. https://foxhugh.com/divination/sun-and-moon-sign-combinations/

Moon, J. (2017, November 23). Sun-Moon astrology combinations. Astroligion.com. https://astroligion.com/sun-moon-astrology-combinations/

Sesay, A. (2020, November 18). Balancing the light and dark: Understanding your sun and moon in astrology. Byrdie. https://www.byrdie.com/astrology-sun-and-moon-5086414

Stardust, L. (2021, November 11). Air signs can talk, think, and network faster than the wind. Cosmopolitan. https://www.cosmopolitan.com/lifestyle/a33314375/air-signs-astrology/

Sun & Moon Combinations: How Well do your Sun & Moon get Along? (n.d.). South Florida Astrologer - Personality & Relationship Astrology https://www.southfloridaastrologer.com/sun--moon-combinations-how-well-do-your-sun--moon-get-along.html

Sun Moon combinations. (n.d.). I. TheHoroscope.Co. https://i.thehoroscope.co/astrology/sun-moon/

Denise. (2018a, September 16). Sagittarius Sun Aries Moon: A demanding personality. I. TheHoroscope.Co. https://i.thehoroscope.co/sagittarius-sun-aries-moon-a-demanding-personality/

Denise. (2018b, September 16). Sagittarius Sun Leo Moon: An honorable personality. I. TheHoroscope.Co. https://i.thehoroscope.co/sagittarius-sun-leo-moon-an-honorable-personality/

Denise. (2018c, October 3). Leo Sun Aries Moon: A Frank personality. I. TheHoroscope.Co. https://i.thehoroscope.co/leo-sun-aries-moon-a-frank-personality/

Denise. (2018d, October 3). Leo Sun Leo Moon: A proud personality. I. TheHoroscope.Co. https://i.thehoroscope.co/leo-sun-leo-moon-a-proud-personality/

Denise. (2018e, October 3). Leo Sun Sagittarius Moon: An inspirational personality. I. TheHoroscope.Co. https://i.thehoroscope.co/leo-sun-sagittarius-moon-an-inspirational-personality/

Denise. (2018f, October 15). Aries Sun Aries Moon: An admirable personality. I. TheHoroscope.Co. https://i.thehoroscope.co/aries-sun-aries-moon-an-admirable-personality/

Denise. (2018g, October 15). Aries Sun Leo Moon: A confident personality. I. TheHoroscope.Co. https://i.thehoroscope.co/aries-sun-leo-moon-a-confident-personality/

Denise. (2018h, October 15). Aries Sun Sagittarius Moon: A decisive personality. I. TheHoroscope.Co. https://i.thehoroscope.co/aries-sun-sagittarius-moon-a-decisive-personality/

Facebook, H. F., Iii. (2011, January 24). Astrology Western Sun and Moon sign combinations. Hugh Fox III. https://foxhugh.com/divination/sun-and-moon-sign-combinations/

Moon, J. (2017, November 23). Sun-Moon astrology combinations. Astroligion.com. https://astroligion.com/sun-moon-astrology-combinations/

Moon, J. (2018a, February 23). Leo sun Aries moon personality. Astroligion.com. https://astroligion.com/leo-sun-aries-moon-personality/

Moon, J. (2018b, February 23). Leo sun Leo moon personality. Astroligion.com. https://astroligion.com/leo-sun-leo-moon-personality/

Moon, J. (2018c, February 23). Leo sun Sagittarius moon personality. Astroligion.com. https://astroligion.com/leo-sun-sagittarius-moon-personality/

Moon, J. (2018d, October 22). Sagittarius sun Aries moon personality. Astroligion.com. https://astroligion.com/sagittarius-sun-aries-moon/

Moon, J. (2018e, October 22). Sagittarius sun Leo moon personality. Astroligion.com. https://astroligion.com/sagittarius-sun-leo-moon/

Moon, J. (2019a, March 17). Aries Sun Leo Moon personality. Astroligion.com. https://astroligion.com/aries-sun-leo-moon/

Moon, J. (2019b, March 17). Aries Sun Sagittarius Moon personality. Astroligion.com. https://astroligion.com/aries-sun-sagittarius-moon/

Sun in Aries & moon in signs. (n.d.). I. TheHoroscope.Co. https://i.thehoroscope.co/astrology/sun-moon/sun-in-aries/

Sun in Leo & moon in signs. (n.d.). I. TheHoroscope.Co. https://i.thehoroscope.co/astrology/sun-moon/sun-in-leo/

Sun in Sagittarius & moon in signs. (n.d.). I. TheHoroscope.Co. https://i.thehoroscope.co/astrology/sun-moon/sun-in-sagittarius/

Sun Moon combinations. (n.d.). I. TheHoroscope.Co. https://i.thehoroscope.co/astrology/sun-moon/

Kelly, A. (2018, February 2). 12 Zodiac Signs: Dates and Personality Traits of Each Star Sign. Allure. https://www.allure.com/story/zodiac-sign-personality-traits-dates